Slotralogy

How to Change Your Habits of Thought

Adam Khan

Published by: YouMe Works
Printed in the United States

Slotralogy © Copyright 2012 by Adam Khan
All rights reserved.

Cover photo © Copyright 2012 by Klassy Evans
All rights reserved.

ISBN-13: 978-1623810009
ISBN-10: 1623810000

If you ever have any questions or comments about anything in this book, or anything at all, I encourage you to email me at: adamkhan@usa.com

Table of Contents

Slotralogy 101 1

Slotralogy 201 8

Changing Thought Habits 12

Practice Clear and Simple Slotras 15

Build Up To It 18

How to Change Your State of Mind 23

Think of Slotras as Training 28

Slotralogy and Positive Thinking 34

Love is a Great Motivator 38

How to Create Serendipity 41

Different Kinds of Motivation 46

How Habits Work 49

How to Form New Habits of Thought 54

The Slotralogy of Motivation and Focus 68

Changing Mental Habits 79

Creating a Purpose Slotra 83

The Magic of Motivation 89

When You Backslide 92

Talking to Yourself For Fun and Profit 94

Unremitting Resolution 103

Never Give Up 108

About the Author 145

Slotralogy 101

YOU THINK the way you think because that's the way you *learned* to think. You look at things the way you're *used to* — the way you've learned over your lifetime to look at things. It seems to you that any sensible person would see things the way you see them. You interpret events in a way that seems natural to you.

But why does it "seem natural?" A person from a different culture might interpret any given event very differently. And not because they are ignorant and you are all-knowing. Someone who knows far more than you may indeed interpret the event very differently than you do.

Okay, you get it. You may be surprised to find some very good news embedded in this fact, however, because it means if you practice thinking a different way, that new way of thinking could *become* natural.

For example, when I first started giving public speeches to promote my books, people weren't listening the way I wanted them to listen. They were listening casually, as if they were watching a sitcom on television. But I was talking about an important subject that could have an enormous impact on the rest of their lives.

My natural way of thinking about their lack of seriousness was demoralizing: "People don't care, I'll never be a good speaker, etc."

But I came up with a new way of thinking about it. I said to myself, "I'm going to *make* them get how important this is!"

I tried lots of different statements, but that one made me the feel most motivated.

Once I came up with this new statement, did I think it *automatically* from then on? No. Not a chance. If I hadn't made a deliberate effort to say that statement to myself whenever I thought about speaking, it would have faded away, and my insight would have vanished into a vague memory. It would not have changed anything.

So I said the statement to myself many times. I wrote it down and carried the piece of paper around with me to remind me to say it, and I got in the habit of saying it to myself whenever I thought about an upcoming speech (and as the speech got closer, that was several times a day).

I would imagine being in front of the audience and I would say to myself with feeling, "I will *make* them get how important this is!" I imagined the phrase coming into my mind during my speech.

After awhile, it became natural to think that way.

That's a demonstration of the tool we're going to explore in this book: To *practice* thinking something until it becomes natural.

This is probably the most basic mental tool in existence. When you want to change the way you *see* things, when you want to change the way you *feel* about something, when you want to treat people differently or have more persistence or eat less, this mental tool is the most fundamental and the most practical. It's like a knife.

A knife is a very simple tool. It is about as basic as tools get. The design hasn't changed much in *thousands* of years, and yet with all our technology and scientific advancement, today in the 21st century when you want to slice a tomato, you probably use a simple knife.

The tool we will be discussing in this book is as ancient and basic as a knife, but we don't really have a good name for it. It's not exactly a slogan or a motto or a mantra or a saying or a proverb or an affirmation, but it's kind of like all of those. So I'm going to coin a word just so we have something to call it. Sorry about doing this, but I think it needs to be done.

I'm going to call it a "slotra." Think of it as a cross between a slogan, which is a phrase used in advertising or politics, and a mantra, which is a word or sound repeated over and over in meditation. But a slotra is neither of those.

A slotra is a phrase or statement you say to yourself many times so the phrase or statement becomes comfortable and familiar and you get good at thinking it. You repeat it *often* enough or *long* enough that eventually the statement comes into your mind on its own and when it's appropriate.

A slotra is a thought you are learning to think. You repeat it the same way and for the same reason you repeat foreign language phrases when you're trying to learn a different language.

When you want to travel to Germany, certain phrases will be handy, so you learn them. And you don't just say a phrase once and expect your brain to remember it when you need it. You say it again and again until it becomes comfortable and familiar. You *practice* saying it so it will come to mind easily when you need it.

That's exactly what to do with slotras.

Each word of a new language feels clumsy to say at first, and you find it hard to pronounce and hard to remember. But the more you say it, the more you *repeat* it, the more natural it feels.

That's the purpose of "slotralogy" — to make helpful thoughts come to mind easily and naturally when you need them. The new thoughts may feel clumsy and awkward to think at first. But if you keep practicing, after awhile they feel more natural.

A Multipurpose Tool

Many different kinds of thoughts can be slotras. For example, you can take a reframe and turn it into a slotra. You can take an insight you've had, encapsulate the insight into a short statement, and say that statement to yourself several times a day for a month. The insight will become familiar and come to mind easily. You've turned your insight into a slotra.

You can make a goal or purpose into a slotra. That's a good one. It keeps your mind focused. That's what I did with my slotra, "I will *make* them get how important this is." It's a *purpose*. That thought, going through my mind, focused my attention on a purpose — a purpose that helped me communicate with more vigor and intensity.

Another good form of slotra is a *rule*. We'll get into that later.

The most useful slotras make you feel a certain emotion, like confidence or motivation or determination. The best slotras I've made were created by starting with the emotion I wanted. I thought first about what I wanted to *feel* in a certain situation.

For example, right after I published my first book, I went around visiting bookstores and asking them to carry my book. I felt nervous and a little awkward when I was introducing myself to the manager, and I didn't like feeling that way, so I thought about what I *wanted* to feel in that situation. I wanted to enjoy it and have fun with it. I wanted to feel relaxed and at ease.

That's step one. Decide what you want to *feel*. The next step is to create a statement that helps you feel that way, that directs your attention in a way that results in the feeling you want. I came up with this one: "I'm going to have fun with this."

Whenever I thought about going into bookstores, I said that phrase and imagined having fun. And as I walked into a bookstore, I made sure that's what was going through my mind. And it worked. I had fun.

You can consider that a two-step formula for creating a slotra:

1. Decide what emotion you want to feel in a particular situation.

2. Come up with a phrase or statement that makes you feel that way in that situation.

A slotra is a kind of on-the-run *motivator*. It's a focuser. A confidence-builder. An anti-negativity shield. It's a mental tool. It gets your mind to work *for* you instead of *against* you.

When I first started promoting my book to bookstores, I would call up a store to get their fax number, the name of the buyer, etc. Most of the time the people on the phone were cooperative and helpful and friendly. But once in awhile, someone would be suspicious and uncooperative. I became downhearted after these calls and didn't want to do them any more.

The negative calls really stuck out in my mind, of course, because of the brain's negative bias. The thoughts going through my head were something like this: "What am I doing this for? I'll never make it. With people like that out there, nobody is going to want my book. They think I'm a pushy salesman. They aren't going to want to listen to me..."

This stream of automatic thoughts made me feel bad. But I talked some sense into myself. "The next time I have a negative person on the line," I told myself, "I'll turn them around. I'll make them like me. They won't be able to resist my charm..."

That last line really struck me as funny, and made me feel strong. It put me in a good mood, so I used it as a slotra. "They won't be able to resist my charm." I said it many times for practice, and when I got on the phone, I deliberately said it to myself, and it worked great. It put me in just the right mood.

I also used "I'll turn it around" quite a bit too. When I felt worried that the next person I called was going to be negative, I kept saying to myself, "It doesn't matter. I'll just turn it around!" The slotra changed my focus from a fear things would go wrong to what I could do about it if it did. The slotra gave me confidence and helped me relax and I actually *was* able to turn it around when I talked to a negative person — because I was in the right mood.

I practiced the phrases many times, and when the right circumstances came up, those phrases came to mind without any effort on my part. They became the content of my mind. They became a natural part of my stream of consciousness. And they helped me get the job done a lot better than the overly negative and emotional thought-stream I originally had. Slotralogy works.

For the next few chapters, we're going to explore slotralogy: What it is, what it isn't, and how you can use it to help you increase your persistence, strengthen your determination, and restore your lost motivation.

Slotralogy 201

AROUND THE TIME I was learning to use slotralogy to promote my first book, my teenage son was looking for a job. I was telling him about slotralogy, and he used it. And instead of just getting the first job he could find, I suggested he first think about what his *ideal* job would be, and *aim for that*, and then use slotras to give himself confidence in the interviews.

A short while later, he told me he'd used slotralogy and landed the perfect job — at Victoria's Secret! He was the only male who worked there (he worked in the stock room), and I don't think he's ever enjoyed a job more.

You can use slotras to give you confidence or *any* emotion you think would be helpful. You can also use straightforward *instructions* as slotras. Michael Johnson, the gold medal Olympian and at one time the fastest man in the world, coached himself before every race, saying things like this to himself: "Stay low. Ease up at the turn." He practiced thinking these things so they came to mind before and during a race. His slotras were instructions and reminders, which was good stuff to think at the right time. He told himself the best way to run the race, or he coached himself to focus on the particular things he was working on.

If you have ever wondered what's going through their heads when great athletes are getting ready for an event, now you know what at least one of them does. And you can use the same method.

Do you have a challenging event coming up soon? Think about what instructions you'd like running through *your* head right before and during that event. Write out a list of ideas. Pick the best one or two, and shorten them into brief statements.

Now practice thinking those slotras. *Practice*. Write them on a card and keep the card with you. Two or three times a day, pull out your card. Practice saying those statements to yourself twenty times each while thinking about the upcoming event. Imagine being at the event and thinking those thoughts.

You're not doing this as some sort of magical incantation, and you're not doing it to "influence your subconscious mind." You're simply *practicing*. You're making those particular thoughts familiar and easy to think.

So *instructions* can work well as slotras. Motivational statements work well too. This principle is for people with an important and challenging purpose, so motivation is an important issue. People with easy, unchallenging goals don't need much motivation or determination.

But you've got something big to accomplish, don't you? And it's *important* to you. So making sure you stay motivated is vital.

To make a motivational slotra, ask yourself these questions: What thoughts put the fight *in* you? What thoughts make you want to try *harder*? What thoughts *fire you up?*

When I started promoting my first book and I ran into setbacks and started to feel discouraged, I used to say to myself, "The world *needs* this!" It made me feel determined and motivated.

Use whatever works.

Practicing those powerful, motivating thoughts is really the key. You can have brilliant insights galore, but if those insights don't occur to you at the time you actually *need* them, they aren't worth much.

Think about it. How many times have you gotten a new understanding, but when the time came to put your insight into action, you thought and acted the same way you always have?

Why do you suppose that happens?

It happens because your new understanding didn't transfer to where you needed it. You didn't remember to think the new thoughts (your new insights) *when you needed to think them.*

You have already-existing thought habits, and those are the thoughts that will go through your mind until you create new thought habits.

How do you create new thought habits? The most basic and simple way is to simply *practice new thoughts* until they come to mind easily and automatically.

Another advantage of repeating your slotra every day is that it keeps the new thought fresh in your mind, which means it'll be right there when the right situation arises.

Having your new insight freshly in mind makes it *much* easier to think that thought at the right time, every time. Do that a few times and what was once a startling new insight will become "just the way you usually think."

Changing Thought Habits

SLOTRAS ARE *especially* practical in situations you know will happen again. Create slotras for situations when you have the same argument with the same person again and again, or the same thoughts after the same golf slice, or the same explanations for why your client said no. Use slotras for situations where you'd like to *change* the way you usually respond.

You can change your thinking with this simple tool. You can make your insights stick. You can make your new ways of thinking *change the way you react* to those tired situations.

The next time a similar situation happens — a situation that used to make you think negatively — you can have your new way of thinking replace the old mental habit. Slotras are especially good at answering this need.

You can think of this as training. A good analogy Tom Miller (author of *Self-Discipline and Emotional Control*) uses in his corporate-training seminars is that your mind is like a horse. If you've ever ridden one of those rented horses that follow a certain path every day, you can get a sense of how your mind works and what it takes to change the way you think.

On a rented horse, it doesn't really matter if you pay attention to where you're going. The *horse* knows where to go. You can just relax and enjoy the scenery. The horse has done it a thousand times before.

In the same way, when your spouse gets that certain look on her face, you have the same thought you have had a thousand times before. You don't have to *figure out* how to interpret her look. You don't have to *figure out* what to feel. Just like the horse, your mind will go where it has gone a thousand times before.

But let's say you want to take a *different* path on the horse. What would you do? At a fork in the road the horse usually goes right. It has *always* gone right, but you've decided going left at the fork is the best way now. You've had an insight and now you know going left is the best way. But every time you come to that fork and *aren't paying attention*, what happens? The horse will go right.

It is not enough to "know" it is better to go left. You actually have to think of it *when you are at the fork*. Remembering an hour later doesn't help.

When you've thought the same way many times, your mind is like that horse. It knows where to go and you don't even have to pay attention to it. But if you want to go a *different* way, you have to do it deliberately.

You have to remember to think the new way when the right time comes. The insight isn't enough. "Knowing" the better way isn't enough. If you're not paying attention, or if your brain doesn't really have any other well-practiced option than the old way, that's the way it will go.

If you have always thought angry thoughts when your child spills something, that's what you'll do next time unless you *remember* your new insight the moment your child spills something.

It may work perfectly well to take a deep breath when you're anxious but the method doesn't do you any good unless you *remember* to use it when you're anxious! Five minutes later may be too late.

That's where slotras come in. A slotra takes your new conclusions and places a sign at the fork in the road, so you can remember to steer your horse down the new path when you come to it. The whole idea of a slotra is to put the new thought where you need it.

Ideally, the *circumstance* will trigger the new thought. The situation will act as a reminder to think the new thought.

How? By practicing saying your slotra over and over *while thinking of situations* where you want the slotra to come to mind.

Practice Clear and Simple Slotras

WHEN Dougal Robertson was in his life raft after killer whales sank their sailboat and left them stranded in the middle of the Pacific Ocean, he realized he was responsible for the lives of his family. Their situation was dire, but he stayed level-headed and continually made good decisions. How did he do it?

He often repeated a phrase to himself. It focused his mind on his purpose. He originally heard the phrase from his wife right after their sailboat sank. Dougal's mind was spiraling down into despair when his wife, Lyn, put her hand on his arm and looked at him. "We must get these boys to land," she said.

It was so simple, but completely clear. And it was *motivating*. That's the very definition of a good slotra.

All five of the people in the life raft used another slotra. Every morning whoever was on watch said,

"What's the password for the day?" And everyone else answered with feeling: "Survival!"

A slotra is *not* something you're trying to hypnotize yourself into believing. And it is not an attempt to sink a suggestion into your "subconscious mind." And it is not for the purpose of influencing the "ether" with your "vibrations of thought." It's not an affirmation.

Slotralogy is thought practice, pure and simple. You are trying to practice thinking certain things so they become familiar and comfortable and natural, and so your new way of thinking comes to mind when you need it.

It helps make your slotras feel comfortable when you make them short, tight, and memorable, because most of the time when you need a new way of thinking, you're busy *doing* something. It's not too often you really need help when you're just sitting around thinking. You need help in the middle of a situation, so you will not want to try to remember anything complicated. You need something brief, preferably with some emotional punch.

Tweak your phrases or statements until they *exactly* suit you, feel right, and fit you. Rearrange your statements and try out different words, until your slotra says exactly what you want it to say, and says it the way you want.

It's best if you only have one or two slotras you are practicing at a time. Practice those for as long as it takes to make them feel natural. You know you've practiced enough when *several* times the thought automatically comes into your mind when you need it. Then pick another one or two to practice.

And when I say "practice," I mean literally saying your slotra to yourself over and over. And say it with *feeling*, even if you're just saying it silently to yourself. Your tone of voice has an influence, even inside your head. If you can get away with it, practice your slotras aloud with feeling.

Dig that groove deep into your brain. Make that pathway in your brain easy to go down.

Write your slotras on cards. You might even have them professionally printed or engraved. Carry your cards with you. This will help you remember to practice them.

Repeat your slotras over and over, forging them into powerful, naturally-occurring thoughts that will serve you for the rest of your life.

I get some of my slotras imprinted on military-style dog tags and wear them around my neck. It's a great way to remind myself of the phrases I'm practice-ing. If this seems a little fanatical, you don't quite understand what a huge difference your thoughts can make.

The thoughts going through your head influence your feelings and behavior at any given moment. And your behavior will largely determine your future. Your thoughts are the rudder. They move the whole thing.

Make sure they're moving you where you want to go.

Build Up To It

IF YOU HAVE a few minutes, a good way to change the way you feel is to say your slotra with only as much feeling as you can muster. Then say it again with a little more feeling. Then again, and again, even more emphatically. It becomes easier and easier to say it with feeling. This can raise you up into the right frame of mind very quickly.

Escalate the slotra when you say it, each repetition more emphatic than the last, louder than the last, more emotional than the last.

You can see a good demonstration of this in the movie, *The Edge*, starring Anthony Hopkins and Alec Baldwin. The two men were out in the Alaskan wilderness. Their plane had crashed and they were trying to get back to civilization. But a huge bear was stalking them. The bear had already brutally killed and *eaten* one of their friends while they looked on helplessly. Now it was after them. Their state of mind was stark terror.

They made a circle of fire which was keeping the bear at bay for the moment, but they had no food or water, and they were running out of wood, so they couldn't stay where they were. The bear was faster than they were so they couldn't outrun it.

In this scene, Bob (Baldwin) has a look of hopeless despair on his face. Charles (Hopkins) is sharpening a long pole, saying he's going to kill the bear. We, the audience, realize this is really the only way out of their predicament. They have to kill it or it will kill them. They can't run. They can't hide. They cannot survive if they only play defense. They're going to have to go on the offensive.

But Bob is in anguish. He doesn't think it's possible. It is an enormous bear.

Bob says, "We can't kill the bear, Charles. He's ahead of us all the time. It's like he's reading our minds — he's *stalking* us for God's sake!" He drops his head. His face has a look of intense anguish. He looks like he's on the verge of crying. You can tell what he's picturing in his mind: The horror of being eaten alive and the despair of realizing there's no way he can avoid this unthinkable nightmare.

Charles says, "You want to die out here, huh? Well, then die. I'll tell you what: *I'm* not going to die. No sir. I'm *not* going to die. I'm going to kill the bear."

Charles looks at Bob. They're in this together. And their lives are at stake.

"Say it," Charles demands. "Say I'm going to kill the bear. Say it!" Charles asks him again. Bob remains silent. Charles yells at him, "Say it! Say *I'm going to kill the bear!*"

Bob, not looking at all convinced, says quietly and without any conviction, "I'm going to kill the bear."

"Say it again," says Charles.

Bob says it a little louder, "I'm going to kill the bear."

"And again!"

This time Bob yells out with a good deal more conviction: "I'M GOING TO KILL THE BEAR!"

"Good! What one man can do, another can do." Charles is yelling at Bob now, like a coach on the sidelines.

Bob repeats, "What one man can do, another can do."

Charles makes him repeat *this* statement a few more times, with increasing feeling, and you see the hopeless despair on Bob's face slowly transform into grim determination.

This is a very useful and powerful transition to make in a circumstance like that. It is just a movie but the actors are demonstrating something quite real.

The thoughts you think in a crisis can save your life or bury you. No kidding. Read the stories of people who have survived seemingly hopeless situations — *Alive: The Story of the Andes Survivors*, the true story of a Rugby team that crashed in the Andes mountains; *Adrift: Seventy-six Days Lost at Sea*, the true story of a sailor who drifted alone on his life raft after his boat sunk; *Endurance: Shackleton's Incredible Voyage*, the true story of a team of Antarctic explorers led by Earnest Shackleton — they all survived because at least one person among them was able to say to himself with firm determination, "We're going to do whatever we *must* to survive." At least one person did not succumb to the despair that naturally occurs to everyone.

Thousands of people have perished in similar circumstances — people who threw up their hands in hopelessness and declared, "We're dead!" — people who wrung their hands and repeated to themselves how hopeless and horrible it was. Those people didn't take the steps that might have saved them.

Remember this in case you are ever in a seriously dangerous predicament.

But you don't have to be in really bad straits to use this. This is a *tool*. A *mental* tool. It's simple and it's good for a great many applications.

No matter how high-tech we get, some tools will never change and will always be useful. People have used axes to chop wood for thousands of years, and in all that time, the basic design hasn't changed. It's basic. It's simple. And it does the job.

You can use this mental tool — making a statement to yourself with feeling, and gradually building up the emotional expression of it — whenever you want to change your state of mind. You can use it whenever the state of mind you have fallen into is counterproductive.

My wife and I got into an argument one night as she was getting ready for bed. I went into the other room so she could sleep. But I knew she wouldn't be able to sleep, and I was feeling too angry and self-righteous to try to help her feel better.

My state of mind wasn't what I wanted it to be. So I changed it. And I had an effective tool that could do the job. First I said to myself, "I can get out of this self-righteous state." I said it quietly at first. Then I said it with a little more feeling. Then I said it with even *more* feeling.

That's always a good way to approach it. Sometimes at first you can't really work up any feeling for it. But if you just say it, even in a monotone, the next time you say it, you can say it with a little more feeling.

I was doing this in my head, by the way. You can say things to *yourself* with feeling. The voice in your head has a tone of voice (and a volume).

Then I said to myself (with no conviction at all), "I'm going to go in there and make her feel good." I wanted her to be able to go to sleep.

I said it again and again, with more feeling every time. And...it changed my state. I was angry to start with. After spending only about six or seven minutes using this mental tool, I changed my state from anger to a firm determination to make her feel good.

I went into the bedroom, hugged her gently, and told her I loved her. She hugged me back and thanked me.

You are not a victim to your own feelings. You can control how you feel if you have the right tool. It's like chopping down a tree — if you have the right tool (an ax, for example) you can do it. If you don't have the right tool, it is nearly impossible.

Can you change your emotional state when you want? Yes, you can, if you have the right tool. Without the right tool, it is nearly impossible.

How to Change Your State of Mind

A FEW YEARS ago, I went to a big event at the Key Arena in Seattle. Tony Robbins was the main speaker and master of ceremonies, but it was an all-day event and many speakers were on the roster. Brian Tracy, the author of some of my favorite audio programs (including *The Psychology of Achievement*), was one of the people giving a talk that day.

Most of the speakers talked about changing your state of mind. This was a "motivational seminar" and I enjoyed it tremendously.

But after it was over I thought, "Here are the best motivational speakers in the world — corporations pay them *thousands* of dollars to talk to the company's top executives because what these guys teach is so *valuable* — and the principles they talk about are the same ones Napoleon Hill wrote about in *Think and Grow Rich* seventy years ago!"

At first I was disappointed. I thought after all these years they should have come up with something new and better.

But then I realized *the same few principles* that worked on human minds seventy years ago still work on human minds today. People haven't really changed. We're still human. What will change your state of mind is exactly the same thing that could change your grandfather's state of mind.

One of the principles Tony talked about was what he called "incantations." That means changing your state of mind by saying positive things to yourself with feeling. Napoleon Hill called it "autosuggestion."

This is the same principle as "thought practice." This is slotralogy. The only thing that has changed in the last seventy years is the *explanation* of why it works.

Napoleon Hill believed that your "vibrations of thought" could influence the world and other people and your own subconscious and that's why it worked so well. Now the explanation is "you are practicing a thought until it comes naturally to mind." The "how to" is the same and it still works, regardless of *why* we think it works.

Although the *principle* has not changed, we *have* learned a few things about how to make it work better. The most important of these is the value of your facial expressions.

Use Your Face

Paul Ekman, author of *What the Face Reveals*, has been studying facial expressions for a long time. He and his colleagues have created a detailed catalog of 43 "facial-action" combinations. They know exactly which tiny muscles are used in any facial expression, and their system of identifying facial expressions is now the standard used in many different fields, including psychology and criminal science. Ekman literally has facial expressions down to a science.

As a key part of the process of finding out which muscles are used in which facial expressions, one day Ekman spent a long time at the lab trying to reproduce an authentic look of sadness on his own face. When he got home that evening he realized he felt depressed.

Ekman explored this further and found when he made his facial muscles create an authentic smile, it *improved* his mood.

Another researcher, Patricia Ruselli, did an experiment completely unrelated to Ekman's work, but got similar results. Ruselli asked volunteers to watch a slide presentation designed to produce sadness. Half the subjects were told to frown while they watched it. The other half were told *not* to frown.

For several hours afterwards, the people who frowned felt more depressed than the people who didn't frown.

Fritz Strack, a psychologist at Mannheim University in Germany, took a group of volunteers and told them he was going to test their physical skills. He showed them a series of cartoons and told them to rate the cartoons' funniness. But they had to hold a pen in their mouths while they did it. Half of them were told to hold it between their lips. The other half had to hold it between their teeth.

The ones with the pen between their teeth rated the cartoons as funnier.

Apparently, when they held the pen between their lips, they couldn't smile, but when it was between their teeth, the pen forced at least some of their facial muscles into a smile, and that small change affected how funny the cartoons seemed to them.

Still another bit of evidence comes from a pilot study that found when people were injected with Botox to get rid of furrowed brows, it improved their mood — it especially reduced symptoms of depression.

Even when your facial expression is changed with a paralyzing toxin, it can alter your emotional state.

The point of all this is to realize that when you change your facial expression, you influence your feelings.

Use this fact. When you practice your slotras, say them with feeling — feeling in your voice and with emotion on your face.

In *Henry V*, Shakespeare displayed his knowledge of human nature, as he did in so many of his plays. While preparing for another attack on a city, King Henry addressed his troops. He gave his men detailed instructions on what to do with their facial expressions (and their breathing). In Act III, Scene I, King Henry said:

> Stiffen the sinews, summon up the blood,
> Disguise fair nature with hard-favour'd rage;
> Then lend the eye a terrible aspect;
> Let it pry through the portage of the head
> Like the brass cannon; let the brow o'erwhelm it
> As fearfully as doth a galled rock
> O'erhang and jutty his confounded base,
> Swill'd with the wild and wasteful ocean.
> Now set the teeth and stretch the nostril wide;
> Hold hard the breath, and bend up every spirit
> To its full height!

Basically, King Henry is telling his soldiers exactly how to get their body and face in a good fighting spirit. He tells them how to change their face and body so they feel more courageous and aggressive.

King Henry instructs his men to make themselves tense and hardened, to put a look of rage on their faces, to make their eyebrows low with their eyes glaring out intensely. He tells them to grit their teeth, flare their nostrils, and to blow out forcefully when they breathe out.

If you do this, even while sitting here reading, you will notice it *does*, in fact, make you feel more aggressive, more grimly determined, more ready to fight.

Repeating a slotra is the most basic principle for taking advantage of the awesome power of your mind and fulfilling your potential. But when you use it, *remember your face*. Say your slotras *with feeling*. And use your tone of voice, your face, your body's posture, and your breathing to help you *intensify* those feelings.

Think of Slotras as Training

THERE ARE two ways you can use slotras. One is to change your state in preparation for a task you are just *about* to do. The other way is *training*. Repeat things to yourself you would like to be in the *habit* of thinking.

A good place to practice slotras is in your car. You can say them out loud with as much feeling as you want without scaring anyone.

Repeat things you would like to get in the habit of thinking. Over time, those phrases will feel more natural to you and come to mind when you need them.

Even this idea isn't new. Napoleon Hill and W. Clement Stone suggested it in their classic book, *Success Through A Positive Mental Attitude*. They called phrases you repeat to yourself "self-starters." They recommended you say statements to yourself over and over rapidly. One of their self-starters is, "Do it now! Do it now! Do it now!"

They suggested saying a statement to yourself fifty times in a row every morning. And what will happen? That thought will into your mind when you need it. The tool is easy to use and works beautifully. As Napoleon Hill wrote:

> Follow the instructions, no matter how abstract or impractical they may, at first, appear to be. The time will soon come, if you do as you have been instructed, in spirit as well as in act, when a whole new universe of power will unfold to you.

You can change your state with this potent mental tool. You can turn despair into determination, wishy-washiness into resolve, anxiety into courage, anger into compassion. This is not one of many basic tools. This is one of very *few* basic tools, and this is one you'll find extremely useful.

You can take over your own thoughts any time. You're not the victim of what goes through your head, or at least you don't have to be at any moment.

One thing this tool can be used for is to put your focus on a purpose or the task at hand. Concentration is often a crucial element in creating a successful outcome. The statement, "I'm going to kill the bear," would not only give the men courage, it would focus their minds on a clear purpose.

Figure out ahead of time what you want to go through your mind in a particular type of circumstance. Practice the thought when you don't need it. This makes the thought easier to think when you do need it. *Practice* the thought. Make it smooth. Make it natural.

Create-a-Slotra-Exercise

1. Think of a situation where you'd like to feel more focused or motivated, or to feel differently than you usually do in that situation.

2. Now imagine being in that situation, but feeling the way you *want* to feel.

3. Now ask yourself, "What would someone have to be thinking in that situation to feel that way?" What would you have to think to feel that way?

4. Make that thought into a good slotra.

And then, of course, practice that slotra often. You should be using this tool — practicing a new thought — several times a day. Make it a habit. Always have a slotra to practice. It only takes a minute, and you can do it walking, driving, shaving, eating, etc. Practice a new slotra three times a day for a month. More if it is really important. This tool gives you more control over your state of mind, which means your life will go the way you want more often.

The possibility of changing your thoughts is of enormous significance. The difference between someone who is ineffective and has a bad attitude and someone who is effective and has a good attitude is simply *their mental habits*. That's what makes the difference: What kind of thoughts do they think most of the time.

What Would You Like to Feel?

A lot of "positive thinking" books of the old days concentrated on being cheerful and enthusiastic. But there are better states of mind for many situations. How about determined or focused? Or motivated. Open and relaxed. Curious and attentive. Kind and affectionate.

My point is: Don't aim for cheerful and enthusiastic necessarily. Think about what state you really want to be in, and create your slotras to make that state happen. Enthusiasm is not good for every situation.

And you want your slotra to make that state happen. If you're trying to create a slotra that makes you feel motivated, for example, your slotra should *not* be: "Be motivated." Your slotra should *make you feel* motivated. The statement "be motivated" doesn't motivate. Neither does "I want to be motivated." Do you see what I'm getting at? What thought will actually make you *feel* motivated? Make *that* into a slotra. What thoughts put the fight *in* you? What thoughts make you want to try? What thoughts fire you up?

"The world needs this!"
"They can't keep me down!"
"I will come through. I won't let her down!"

Whatever works. Robert E. Peary, the first man to reach the North Pole, tried and failed many times before he succeeded. He had a motto he repeated over and over, especially after his trip where he lost several of his toes: "I will find a way or make one."

Imagine yourself with a goal that means a lot to you but is extremely challenging. And then say to yourself: "I will find a way or make one." Can you feel the determination the slotra gives you? Peary was tirelessly persistent in accomplishing his goal. He tried again and again, overcame tremendous odds and finally reached his goal.

Usually history books don't explain *why* someone is determined. But I'll tell you why: He had a good slotra. Why did others fail or die? Many times it's because they didn't have a good enough slotra, or they didn't have one at all.

What some people don't realize is that determination can be *generated*. It's not like you are either determined or not. You can *create* a state of determination; not for all time, but here in this moment, just as you can't make your spouse feel loved once and for all, but you can definitely do it in the moment and most any moment you choose.

So create a slotra that gives you a feeling of determination. A slotra should direct your attention or change your emotions. Or both. Having an important reason to succeed is motivating — and it allows for strong interpretations of events (that is, interpretations that make you strong, determined and motivated, as opposed to interpretations that make you weak, demoralized, or afraid). So your reason to succeed could be your slotra.

Having an almost continual focus on your clear aim allows your thoughts to be preoccupied with (and always *returning* to) something *positive*, something future-oriented, toward accomplishment and action. This is the most powerful, positive way to protect yourself from negativity.

It's not a coincidence that the most morale-boosting book in history (*Think and Grow Rich*) was written during the Great Depression — which could justifiably be named The Great Demoralization.

A good slotra will aim your attention in a way that creates a positive frame of mind. You can use this tool every day, even several times a day.

The content of your mind makes a huge difference in how well you can overcome obstacles. And how well you overcome obstacles has a large influence on how successful you will be in the long run.

Slotralogy and Positive Thinking

MANY PEOPLE have told me they dislike trying to think positive because it feels forced and phony. They say things to themselves they don't really believe and it doesn't seem to make much difference. Saying these positive things doesn't make them feel any better.

I think cognitive psychology has made an important contribution to this discussion. They've come up with a kind of anti-negativity process. It is *arguing with negative thoughts*. It is a process of discovering mistakes in your negative explanations of setbacks, and it works exceedingly well to change how you feel without feeling phony. Read the book, *Antivirus For Your Mind*, to learn more about this.

And since you already feel negative when you want to change your attitude, it is fairly easy to *do* something negative, like find mistakes in your negative thoughts, to criticize your thoughts, or to aggressively *argue* with your thoughts.

On the other hand, it is exceedingly difficult to say or believe something *positive* when you feel so negative.

After arguing with your negative thoughts for a while, you won't feel so bad, so you'll be in a better state of mind — a state more conductive to doing something more positive, like changing your mindset with a slotra.

Slotralogy is different than positive thinking, although, of course, they overlap a little. The thoughts you're practicing don't necessarily have to be positive or cheery. The purpose is not just to make you feel *positive*, but to direct your attention in a productive, constructive way.

When Dougal Robertson said to himself, "We must get these boys to land," he said it with a kind of grim determination, not cheerfulness or enthusiasm. He would have had to fake any enthusiasm, and it was unnecessary. Grim determination worked just fine and it was way better than despair.

Nelson Mandela describes himself as an optimist. Not a perpetually cheery person, but one who "keeps one's head pointed toward the sun, one's feet moving forward." I like that definition. "There were many dark moments," wrote Mandela, "when my faith in humanity was sorely tested, but I would not and could not give myself up to despair. That way lay defeat and death."

Notice that he didn't give himself up to despair, but not because he was naturally buoyant. His refusal to sink into despair was a *decision*. He saw the practical implications of directing his mind deliberately, and used it. Most survivors of trying conditions (and most successful people) do the same.

Al Siebert, author of the *The Survivor Personality*, puts it this way, "The will to live is different from hopefulness or optimism. The survivors I have interviewed have not talked about being sustained by hope." They are sustained by their *determination*, grim or not.

Optimism is different than hope. One reason optimism can be so powerful is that it is a self-fulfilling prophesy. Or at least it has a tendency to *become* self-fulfilling. Assume something is changeable, assume you can do it, and you're more motivated to try than if you assume you can't or that it is unchangeable.

When Jim Carrey first decided to become a comedian, his father, Percy, helped him out. Percy played the saxophone when he was younger and dreamed of playing it for a vocation, but he gave it up to become an accountant. He didn't want his son to give up *his* dream.

Jim says of his father, "He taught me it's better to go after something special and risk starving to death than to surrender."

Percy found Jim an opportunity to try his talent on stage when Jim was only 15 years old. In a Toronto comedy club, dressed in a yellow polyester suit his mom bought for him, Jim had his first experience entertaining people.

It was a nightmare. The emcee made *Jim* the entertainment by making fun of him the whole time Jim was trying to do his bit.

Jim Carrey, who went on to become one of the most successful entertainers of his time, was so demoralized by this experience, he didn't try again for *two years*.

"I have no idea what motivated me to try again," he said, "I just felt like giving it a shot. Failure isn't the end unless you give up."

Although Jim may not realize what motivated him to try again, he reveals a principle in that last sentence — a statement, a belief that encourages persistence. It would make an excellent slotra. If you have a goal you really care about and you've experienced a setback, try practicing this thought: "Failure isn't the end unless you give up." Excellent.

Love is a Great Motivator

ONE OF the things you can use slotras for is to remind you of what you're striving for — what's your motivation? You've chosen a goal and you are working toward it. Why do you want to achieve it?

Tap into your strongest motivations, including love, pride, anger, etc. It doesn't have to be nice. It doesn't have to sound pretty to others. In fact, nicey-nice thoughts are some of the weakest there are. If you want to be the best "to prove those bastards wrong" and if that's a really strong motivation that gets you going, use it.

For many people, a very strong motivation can be team-oriented — to come through for the *team*, to be the hero, to not let your buddy down.

In interviews with soldiers who have done heroic deeds, most of them say they didn't do it for the "principle of democracy" or to promote the cause of freedom in the world or because it was their duty. What actually motivated the soldier was "I didn't want to let my buddy down." Their fellow Marines were pinned down by a machine gun in a pillbox, for example, and the hero jumps in to stop it because those Marines are his buddies. *He loves those guys*, and love is an extremely powerful motivation.

And your wife is your buddy. Your family is your team. The people you work with are another team. Any organization you participate in is a team. If you are naturally and strongly motivated by your loyalty and commitment to any of these teams, *use* that motivation when you create your slotras. For example:

> She's counting on me. I won't let her down.
> I will come through for my family.
> We must get these boys to land.

Use what gives you strength. That is the number one criteria for choosing your slotra: *It must give you strength.* It must reinforce your determination, and ideally, boost your motivation.

The book, *The Long Walk: The True Story of a Trek to Freedom*, is about how six men escape from a Soviet prison camp in Siberia and walk all the way across the continent to India.

At one point in the story, the men had made it out of Siberia, had walked across the Soviet Union, across the immense Gobi Desert in Mongolia and had entered Tibet. They still had to hike over the Himalayas, and were on the lookout for Chinese soldiers. If they were caught, they were finished. They didn't have any money. They didn't have any passports. Their chances of making it to India would seem remote to the most sanguine optimist. But they didn't spend any time talking about what would happen if they *didn't* make it. As the author, Slavomir Rawicz wrote, "We could not afford to think of failure."

Being so close to the edge of death makes you acutely aware of the impact of your own thoughts. Your thoughts make a *huge* difference, whether you are in a life-or-death struggle, or simply trying to accomplish a financial goal.

Whatever your goal, find thoughts that help you, that motivate you, and *practice* them. Focus on the most motivating impulse you have, and build a slotra to capitalize on it.

How to Create Serendipity

AL SIEBERT spent forty years studying survivors of all kinds — concentration camp survivors, people lost at sea, castaways, prisoners of war, etc. Siebert writes, "They go from being emotionally upset to coping to thriving to serendipity with amazing speed."

How do they do it? One of the most important things they do is use slotras. Siebert has collected lots of questionnaires by survivors, and he says when a survivor hits a setback, "they frequently repeat sayings to themselves," like these:

> When the going gets tough, the tough get going.

> When life hands you a lemon, make lemonade.

And survivors ply themselves with good-quality questions. It works for survivors just as it works for anyone else in any other difficult situation. A life-or-death situation only intensifies the outcome: Those who lived to tell the tale did something successful with their minds. They asked questions like these:

Why is it *good* this happened?

Is there an opportunity here that did not exist before?

What can I do to turn this around and make it turn out well for all of us?

These are great questions. Think about the difference between occupying your mind with the questions above, as opposed to questions that might come more naturally. For example, "Why me?" or "What have I done to deserve this?" or "How could I have been so stupid?"

Thought Practice

The survivors say those slotras or ask those questions *often*. Without realizing what they're doing, they are *practicing* those thoughts, making them familiar and comfortable. Then when they're in a difficult survival situation, those well-practiced thoughts *save them* — keep their mind focused on what needs to be done, keep them trying to survive, keeping them from giving up or killing themselves to end it all.

You can use the same principle in your (probably) less dire circumstances. Say something to yourself that makes you feel motivated. Say what makes you feel strong and determined.

Make a list of statements. Specifically, think of the most common situations where you don't feel motivated (but want to), and try to come up with statements you could say to yourself in those situations that would make you feel motivated or strong or relaxed or whatever you want to feel.

Or think of what you could say to yourself that would make you more *effective*. Just sit down and do the work of thinking up ideas. Write them all down.

Once you have this list, go through and start scratching out the weakest ones. And change the wording on others so they are more motivating. Condense your statements down to mostly single sentences, sometimes phrases, and sometimes two or three sentences if you really feel you must.

Go through the list again and trim it down to the most strength-giving slotras. Now type them up and print them. Fold the paper up and carry it in your pocket. Pull it out three to five times a day, and read each sentence several times *with feeling*.

Sometimes pull it out in those situations where you need motivation, or right *before* you're going to need it, and read each sentence with feeling and see which ones work the best. Keep tweaking the wording and eliminating the weaker ones until you have one or two slotras that give you the best results. Write those two on a card and carry that card everywhere you go.

Every day, five times a day, pull the card out and say those slotras to yourself several times each.

The more you repeat the slotra, the more ingrained it becomes. If you do it twice a day, it may take months before the slotra becomes ingrained and comes to mind easily. If you do it fifty times a day, it will happen very quickly.

The things you think are as much a habit as the way you tie your shoes. You do it a certain way, and it comes automatically. But the ways you think naturally or automatically may not be the most motivating.

Right after I self-published my first book, I was going around visiting bookstores, asking them to stock my book on their shelves, and then coming back later to see how things were going, and I was soon discouraged. I thought the book business was going to be pretty easy and the hard part was writing and publishing the book. I thought people would pick up my book and just go nuts, tell all their friends and my book would have a hard time staying on the shelves because it would be snatched up as soon as it was put out, and I'd be on easy street. But I was starting to realize, "I'm going to have to *work* at it. I'm going to have to do things to get people into the store looking for my book."

I was feeling kind of disheartened by this realization, but then I used one of my slotras: "The world *needs* better attitudes!"

That slotra bucked me up. It renewed my fighting spirit. It kept me working toward my goal and dissolved my discouragement. The phrase motivated me and made me feel determined.

What thoughts put the fight in *you?* What thoughts make you want to *try?* What thoughts fire you up? Make a list, eliminate all but the most effective, and keep editing them until they are powerful thoughts that really get to you, and then *practice* them.

Different Kinds of Motivation

DESIRE IS ONE kind of motivation. Fear is another. If you look at the basic training or "boot camps" of military organizations, you will see that the whole thing is one giant motivational stew. They use anything and everything that will motivate the recruits, and the end result is, these recruits are more motivated than they have ever been or probably ever will be.

For example, the drill sergeants remind the recruits again and again that not everyone is going to make it. Some people won't be able to stick it out and graduate from basic training. For many of the recruits, this motivates them to try to be one of the strong, capable people who make it and avoid being one of the ones who drop out because they can't hack it.

Sometimes when one recruit lags behind or doesn't work hard enough, the rest of his platoon is punished for it. This is another kind of motivation. It is using the recruit's embarrassment and feeling of ethical obligation, as well as using the peer pressure from the rest of the platoon to motivate him to try harder.

If you don't keep up during a run, you might get extra guard duty (rather than badly-needed sleep), or you might have to do push-ups until your chest burns. This is a different kind of motivation — pushing yourself through suffering *now* in order to avoid greater suffering *later*.

Some motivations work better than others, under different circumstances and for different people, so basic training uses them *all* to make sure everyone is motivated, and as motivated as possible.

The different types of motivations can add together without canceling each other out. For example, the peer pressure doesn't cancel out the desire to be one of the chosen few. They add together to make an even more intense overall motivation.

You can use the same principle. When you're thinking up statements to motivate yourself, try out many different *kinds* of motivation. Try to think of anything that works on you. Try *scaring* yourself. Make yourself white-hot with desire. Use embarrassment, peer pressure, lust, curiosity, pride — anything that gets you fired up and working hard.

If it motivates you to be the best, to be better than others, *use* that. You don't have to share these statements with anyone else. This is up to *you* in the privacy of your own mind. It is nobody's business but your own.

So do not limit yourself to motivations or slotras that would be publicly acceptable and politically correct. Appeal to your ego, appeal to your machismo, appeal to your desire to attract a mate — whatever makes you feel motivated.

The bottom line is: Find things to think that make you feel motivated, and practice those thoughts. Get in the *habit* of thinking those things, and you will be a more motivated person.

It's a matter of habit. The difference between a very successful person and an unsuccessful person is mostly their persistence and motivation. And the difference between a persistent, motivated person and a quitter is usually simply their *mental habits*.

In the next chapter, we'll explore the heart of the matter — what habits are, and how they work.

How Habits Work

MAKING a decision is pretty easy. *Sticking with it* is the hard part, mainly because if a habit is already formed, it is difficult to change. For example, I often roll up my shirtsleeves. When it comes time to take off the shirt, I used to just take it off and throw it in the laundry basket.

But I decided to unroll the sleeves first. It makes washing a little easier. It was a small thing, but difficult because I was already in the habit of taking off my shirt and throwing it in the basket without unrolling the sleeves. I had made the same movements in the same sequence hundreds of times. It was so automatic and habitual, I didn't really pay attention while I was doing it. And that's the main reason it was so hard to remember.

Changing the way you think or behave isn't easy. Maybe you've noticed that already. But the reason it is difficult is not that your mind is pigheaded. It is because you're not in the habit of thinking certain things *at certain times*.

Let me be extra clear on this. And please be aware that this is a very important point. Change is not difficult because you "subconsciously resist" or because you "really" don't want to change, or because you're lazy, or because you're stubborn. There is a very simple and quite benign reason change is difficult:

> You are not *in the habit* of thinking certain things at certain times.

Habits are very powerful. And they can work *for* you or *against* you. For example, Jimmy Jones was in jail and wanted to escape. This is a true story. He put himself in a trash bag and might have gotten away with it but when they called his name during roll call, habit took over and he answered, "Here," from inside the bag!

Habit is powerful. And *mental* habits are as firmly rooted as any *physical* habit, like responding to role call. How can you harness the incredible power of habit? Specifically, how can you form the habit of thinking certain things at certain times? How can you make *sure* you'll remember at the right time?

Answer: Make a slotra and practice it. If you want to remember to listen well to your spouse, make a slotra such as: *Listen well or live in hell*. Repeat that slotra to yourself. Make a goal of repeating it, say, ten times a day. Do that for a few weeks and you will form a new habit. Your brain will become accustomed to thinking that thought. The thought will become something you naturally think when you need to. The thought will come to mind easily.

I'm making this sound very easy, and truly it is. But there is a catch: You will get bored and want to move on. When that happens, start thinking of the reasons you really want to do this. Then get back to repeating your slotra.

By repeating the slotra over and over — by repeating the exact words you want to think over and over — the thought gets fixed in your mind and highly available. It's not in the back of your mind. It's right up front and easy to access. So you'll remember it in those key moments, and *that will cause your habits to change.*

I once had the habit of not sticking with things. I tried to change that habit many times, but never stuck with it long enough to get rid of the habit!

After learning how slotralogy works, I chose *stay on track* as my slotra. After repeating that phrase to myself many times a day for only a couple of days, whenever I found myself about to give up on something or go off on a tangent that caught my interest, the words would pop into my mind: *Stay on track.*

It was so handy to have the slotra come into my mind when I needed it. And every time it came to mind, I heeded it. I got back on track.

Of course, when the thought appeared my mind, I *could* have ignored it. But I didn't *want* to ignore it. And you won't either, for the same reason: This is a change you have deliberately chosen. It's something you *want*, and the slotra has come into your mind at the perfect moment.

This isn't unpleasant. This isn't "forcing" yourself to change. I didn't feel at all bothered when the slotra popped up in my thoughts. My feeling was similar to wanting to remember to buy milk at the store, but forgetting. Then a friend who came to the store with me says, "Remember, you wanted to get some milk." I don't feel harassed. Just the opposite. My response is: "Oh yeah! Thanks for reminding me!"

This is a simple technique that works beautifully. To come up with a good slotra, decide what you'd like to go through your head at certain key times.

For example, I was about to walk into a radio station to ask if they would interview me. I thought to myself, "This is going to be fun!" That was my slotra. I had already repeated it to myself many times and it came to mind naturally as I walked up to the door. It relaxed me and made me more effective.

I came up with that slotra by asking myself, "What would I like to go through my mind as I walk into radio stations?" I made a list of possible phrases and chose the best one. Then I practiced thinking that phrase — saying it to myself many times a day until it was a natural, comfortable thought that came to mind automatically in those circumstances. This is fairly easy to do.

Some people get lucky and someone does it for them (a parent or a drill sergeant). If you weren't that lucky, you can do it for yourself and design thoughts more closely tailored to what you want.

A slotra is not an affirmation. It's a statement of fact or purpose, or it's a rule you want to follow. Make it short, tight and memorable because most of the time you are *doing* something. Your attention is already occupied with what you're doing. You don't want a slotra so long you have to stop and think about it.

Create your customized slotras and repeat them to yourself, forging them into powerful tools. Then create frequent opportunities to use that tool so you become adept at using it. I'll tell you how to create opportunities in the next chapter.

How to Form New Habits of Thought

DURING World War II, Ted Bengermino was responsible for maintaining records of men killed or missing in action. He often had to take the personal effects of soldiers killed in action and send the things to the young men's parents, and he worried himself sick that his department might make a mistake. What if they accidentally told the wrong parents their son was dead?

Bengermino was tortured by anxiety so often, he started worrying about his own health. He lost thirty-four pounds from worry and exhaustion. He worried he might be a physical wreck when he went home after the war. He cried when he was alone. "There was a period soon after the Battle of the Bulge started," he said, "that I gave up hope of ever being a normal human being again."

He eventually ended up in the Army medical clinic. The doctor examined Ted and concluded his problem was mental. "Ted," he said, "I want you to think of your life as an hourglass…"

The doctor explained the basic truth: We all want to do more in a day than can be done. But we've got to take the tasks one at a time. If we don't, it would be like trying to *force* the grains of sand through the narrow part of the hourglass. We would break under the strain.

The doctor's advice was Ted's turning point. After this session with the doctor, Ted often said to himself, "One grain of sand at a time…One task at a time." That became his slotra. He practiced thinking it. And he began to recover.

After the war, working for a printing company, he sometimes felt pressure and he became anxious and tense. The slotra would come into his mind, "One grain of sand at a time. One task at a time."

"By repeating those words to myself over and over," he said, "I accomplished my tasks in a more efficient manner and I did my work without the confused and jumbled feeling that had almost wrecked me on the battlefield."

When you want to make a change in your life, remember that the key is remembering to think something specific at specific times. To ingrain a thought, make a slotra and repeat it. It's the power tool for change.

Remind Yourself

Miki has been shy her whole life. She feels anxious around people, especially when she feels she's being watched or judged. She feels strongly compelled to make sure people don't disapprove of her. She tries to please everybody and in doing so, she limits her self-expression. She doesn't feel free to be herself. She feels she must make sure everybody is pleased with her.

One day she realizes it's okay if every person is not a hundred percent pleased with her. In fact, it's impossible. She can't please everybody. And she's no longer willing to sacrifice her own integrity and honesty to make others more comfortable.

That's a great insight. Will it make any difference? It could. But tomorrow, when Miki is talking to her father, the old patterns will be there very strongly. She may forget all about her insight. Mental habits are just as automatic as physical habits.

There is one technique that can preserve her insight: She could *remind* herself. Not by writing it in a journal that she may not read until three years from now. Not by thinking about it once or twice. Not by "firmly making up her mind" she will remember. But by taking on the task of reminding herself *like it is important*. How can she remind herself in a way that she cannot ignore or overlook?

This is our task also. We have insights all the time. Will they make any difference? It depends on how successfully we remind ourselves. Of course, you have to be selective. Some of the things you learn aren't worth taking the time to ingrain. But when you find one that *is* worth the time, take the task seriously and do it wholeheartedly. Don't let that insight fade away. Make it real. Let it change your life for the better.

Put the insight on your desktop. Write it on a card and keep it in your pocket. Pull it out and look at it several times a day. Post it on your dashboard, on the refrigerator, on the bathroom mirror. Have it engraved on a pendant and wear it. Record it and listen to it while you drive.

And I'm not talking about doing *one* of these, like some sort of gesture. I mean do them all and anything *else* you can think of. I'm talking about getting serious about remembering your insights!

And here's a hot tip: Your brain stops looking at stationary things. If Miki put a giant poster on her wall that says: "It's okay if every person is not a hundred percent pleased with you," even if the letters are six feet high, within a couple weeks *she won't notice the poster any more.* Her brain will get used to seeing it. Her brain already knows what the poster says and will stop registering it.

That means if you post something on your bathroom mirror, you'll have to move it to another location after a couple days or you will stop noticing it. Or you can ask your spouse to move it for you. Use your ingenuity to come up with novel ways to remind you of the insight. How about paying your children a dollar every time they remind your of your insight?

I remembered to unroll my shirtsleeves the first day I tried, because my decision was fresh in my mind. But then for three days I forgot. Then I reminded myself, and started concentrating on reminding myself, and did it for two days. Then I forgot for a few more. Eventually I formed a new habit. Now I've unrolled those shirtsleeves so many times, it would be difficult to remember to leave them rolled up.

You know how it is. There are lots of things we do automatically like that. We have done them so many times, the sequence of movements doesn't require our attention, so our attention goes to other things while we do it.

For most people, driving a car is like that, which is amazing because driving a car is a complex activity, which anyone first learning to drive is painfully aware of. You have to pay attention to the road, other cars, signs, turns, etc., and move the steering wheel and foot-pedals in response to what you see. There's a lot going on. A lot to remember.

But after driving for a few years, most people can do it all without really paying attention. When something unusual happens, you "wake up" and put your attention on the road, almost as if you took over the manual control of a car driving on "automatic pilot."

If driving conditions are normal, an experienced driver can engage in a conversation with a passenger while the automatic pilot watches and responds to the driving situation. Amazing!

That remarkable level of automatic behavior was created just by doing something many times. But there are some things you've done even *more* often than driving, like tying your shoes. And thinking.

Have you ever seen a child learn to tie his shoes? You have forgotten what a complex task it is. You've done it thousands of times. If you tried to tie your shoes a different way now, you'd have a hard time. Each one of your movements is a cue or a trigger for the next movement in the sequence, and each has been linked together again and again. It's a habit. It happens automatically. And when you're doing it, you don't really pay attention to the task. If you tried doing it differently, you would have to work on it and it wouldn't be easy.

It's the same way with your thoughts. You've had some sequences of thoughts *thousands* of times, often triggered by the same or similar events.

For example, when someone you love has an angry look on her or his face, it may trigger a sequence of thoughts. You've gone through the same sequence of thoughts so many times, you aren't even aware of them any more. All you know is the end result: You feel bad. You might have gone through that same sequence of thoughts since you first began to think.

When you were a child and your parents gave you that look, you first formed your sequence of thoughts, however primitive they were back then.

Those thought-patterns may have been the first complex thoughts you ever had. And if you've never stopped and changed those patterns, you've been going through the same patterns over and over almost your entire life, having the same feelings in response to those same facial expressions.

Then I come along and tell you to pay attention to what you're thinking. But by the time you feel a negative emotion, you've already gone through the sequence of thoughts that got you there. And you did it so quickly, you didn't even know you were thinking. I had a hard enough time becoming aware enough to remember to unroll my shirtsleeves. It's far more difficult to become aware of your thinking when you feel bad.

But while it's true your habits can get you into trouble sometimes, habits are also tremendously useful. *Habits* are not the enemy. Habits are how you hold on to patterns, useful or not. If you weren't able to form habits, life would be much more difficult.

The fact that you can form habits and that those habits are resistant to change is *good* because when you have a useful sequence of thoughts or actions, you won't have to try to remember them every time. You can relax and put your attention on other things.

Because habits are hard to break, you can *gain* something. It's like a ratchet. It allows you to move forward and prevents you from slipping back. So you can get somewhere. You can improve.

The only catch is when you need to *change* a habit that already exists.

Blazing a New Path

A habit or thought pattern is like a well-worn path through a large meadow. If you're going to cross this meadow, the easiest way to do it is by following the path.

But let's say the path takes you to a swamp, and that's not where you want to go anymore. There are berry bushes at the edge of a different part of the meadow, and that's what you want.

The only problem is, there is no path to the berry bushes and the grass in the meadow is four feet high and hard to walk through.

Obviously, the thing you need to do is to *make a new path*. It will be hard. It will be a lot harder than going down the well-worn path to the swamp. But if you want to get to the berry bushes and stop ending up in the swamp, that's what you need to do.

You can start your new path anywhere along the old path — as long as you eventually aim toward the berry bushes.

Your brain is very close to that analogy. When you learn something new, it forms *a pattern of paths* between your brain cells. The more times the same thing goes over the same path, the stronger the signal gets, and the more likely it will fire that way the next time.

For instance, when you first learn a person's name, it's a new pathway in your brain: You're connecting this person's face with the name David. The path is weak: You've only walked to the berry bushes once. When someone asks you what his name is, you have to struggle to remember.

But after awhile, by connecting David's face with his name over and over, the path through your brain becomes well-worn. It's easy for your brain to go down that particular path. It feels like there is no other way to go. If someone asks you, "What's his name?" you automatically say, "David."

In the meadow, let's say you've walked to the berry bushes a couple of times. When you begin down the original path again, you come to a fork in the path: there's a well-worn path that leads to a swamp, and there's another one — rough and difficult to walk on, but visible — that leads to berry bushes.

What happens when you choose the berry bush path *every time* you come to the fork? It becomes easier and easier to walk down.

And what happens to the *other* path? It grows over and becomes more and more difficult to walk down. The same is true for your brain. When a new habit is forming, at some point it will hold without effort. It will become automatic.

For example: Once upon a time, I found it difficult to sit at my computer and write while Klassy, my wife, was in the room. I felt I was being rude. So I did most of my writing late at night after she went to bed, and then slept late.

But I didn't like sleeping away so much of the daylight. I tried to write in the morning, but I let her interrupt me. I felt bad when I told her not to interrupt. She didn't have a problem with it, but while I was writing, I felt bad. It felt as if she must resent me. It was really stupid, but I was young and somehow I had this habit of thinking. It was just a sequence of thoughts. Klassy had no problem with it. It was all in my head.

I knew my life would work better if I wrote in the daytime while Klassy was around. The first time I tried it, I was distracted by feelings of guilt. So I asked myself what I was thinking. My answer: "She resents me. She wants to talk to me but feels shut out. Her feelings are hurt."

I talked some sense into myself: "She already told me she doesn't resent me." And I kept writing. Every time the thoughts came up, I argued with them again. Now they don't come up any more. And I am writing during the day and sleeping at night. It worked quickly because I had several opportunities *every day* to practice.

Opportunities to Practice

I'm sure you've tried to change a habit many times — an eating habit, exercise, the way you communicate, whatever — and at least sometimes you found it difficult. Do you know what made it difficult? It wasn't because you didn't really want to. It wasn't because you didn't try or weren't sincere. It wasn't because you "lacked discipline." It was because the opportunities to practice *were too far apart*. For the love of all that is holy, you must remember this!

Your brain and the meadow work in the same way: If you came by one day and struggled your way across the meadow to the berry bushes and then came back a *month* later, what happened to your preliminary path to the berry bushes? It's gone. It has grown over.

In the same way, when you have an insight — and you know it's a *good* insight and will change your life — and then it comes to nothing, it's because too much time has gone by between the moment of insight and the next opportunity to *use* that insight. When the opportunity finally came, the partially-formed pathway in your brain was gone.

One insight will usually not be enough: It's only one walk through the meadow. It's merely a single pass through a new pattern in your brain.

Have you ever had the frustrating experience of knowing exactly what you need to do to solve a problem or reach a goal only to have time go by without anything coming of your great insight? Well, there was probably nothing wrong with the insight itself. It was just one walk through the meadow.

If you then share your insight to someone else, it's *another* walk through the meadow. If you then write it on a card and post it on your bathroom mirror, that's another walk. If you read it the next morning, that's another walk. And after enough of these walks, a faint path begins to form, and the more times you go down that path, the clearer it becomes.

The more you think your insight, the easier it becomes to think it, the more natural it becomes until eventually it becomes "second nature." At some point, when you look at the meadow, there is only one way to go: There is only one path, and the *other* one has grown over.

Of course, a faster way would be to repeat that thought over and over — fifty, a hundred, two hundred times a day. It would be like walking back and forth on the meadow two hundred times a day. It doesn't take many days to make that thought very easy to think and come to you naturally.

And when thought-habits change, behavior and feeling habits change, and when *those* change, the kinds of results you get change too.

Another good way to establish a new pattern is to *create* opportunities to practice. Don't wait for natural opportunities to happen. Often you can't create opportunities in real life. If you're trying to change the way you react when your spouse gets mad at you, for example, you probably don't want to make your spouse mad at you every day for three weeks so you can lay down a new pattern in your brain. That would be too rough on everyone. But you can practice in your head, and it'll still form a new pattern in your brain. It's just like learning someone's name.

The fastest way to remember a name is to use the person's name a lot and repeat it in your mind the first time you meet her. Every time you say her name to yourself while looking at her face, you're strengthening that pathway in your brain. Saying it to *yourself* and visualizing her face works as well as saying it *out loud* while looking at her face. Mental rehearsal lays down patterns in the brain and nervous system almost as well as real-live practice.

Have you read about the now-famous experiments with basketball players? One group practiced making shots out on the court. Another group practiced making shots in their minds. The ones who mentally rehearsed improved nearly as much as those who practiced in reality. The experiment has been repeated with other tasks with the same results. Making a new pathway in your brain does not require reality. Imagination can do it.

When you try to form a new mental habit with any of the ideas in this book, make sure you practice often enough to form a new pathway. Those opportunities to practice must be close together.

If you're dealing with something that happens every day, it won't be a problem. But if the opportunity to use the new pattern is spaced further apart, then practice it *mentally*: Imagine situations that might happen or have already happened, and then walk yourself through the new pattern several times. Do it again the next day, several times.

Keep this up until you have a real-live opportunity, and if you go down the new pathway automatically, you don't need to practice anymore.

That's how to make new paths in your life.

I want to emphasize that when you practice in your mind, it's important to start *before* the veer-off point. That's the crucial place. The thought habit you already have goes right by that place without stopping. So the most important part of the path to work on is the point of *departure* from the old pattern.

What's going to *remind* you to take a new direction? Practice *that*, and go through the rest of the new path. Follow it all the way to the berry bushes. Try to *never* go down the old path again. Let it grow over and disappear.

For example, I tend to interrupt Klassy when she's talking, and I would like to change that habit. But to change the habit, I have to remember at the right time. So I practice in my mind. I imagine us having a conversation (this is going down the old path) and there is a point where I am at a fork in the road — one way goes to interrupting her. That's the old path. The new path I want to form is *not* interrupting. What will be the reminder? What will trigger me to remember to take the new path? I chose the feeling of wanting to interrupt. So I picture a conversation in my mind's eye, and I imagine having the feeling of wanting to interrupt, and I imagine letting it go and I see her in my mind's eye finishing what she wants to say and feeling happy that she feels heard. And I imagine this over and over again. Then when I'm in a real conversation and I have a feeling of wanting to interrupt, guess what will come to mind automatically?

This is the nuts and bolts of how to make your insights stick. This is how to make a change and hold it. This is how to form new habits. Go over the path enough to make a solid pathway.

One important principle is to focus on one habit at a time. Find *one* insight that will make a big difference, and *focus* on it. Until you have something *specific* to work on, it is very difficult to get anywhere. Work on changing one specific mental habit and make significant progress on it. *Then* go to the next thing.

The Slotralogy of Motivation and Focus

STAYING FOCUSED will help you stay motivated. Sounds easy enough, but it isn't. Distractions and sidetracks are constantly working against you. The skill to learn is to get faster at *noticing* when you're off track.

Significant progress toward a goal you really want is a powerful motivator. The more focused you are, the more progress you'll make, so the more motivated you will feel.

Distractions aren't always negative. Alex Haley, the author of *Roots*, was down and out at one point, living in a cleaned out storage room, barely getting enough to eat while he banged away on his one main possession: A used manual typewriter. Haley wanted to be a writer.

His storage room was cold. It had no bathroom. He was seriously roughing it. He had been trying to make it as a writer for a year or so and he was broke. One day he searched around his house to see how much money he had. All added together, he had 18 cents.

Then out of the blue, a friend called him and offered him a well-paying job as a public information assistant.

At first he was very happy at the idea, but then he realized this was a like a Siren song. He was being lured away from his dream. He did the difficult thing and declined the offer, went back to his cold storage room and banged away on his used typewriter. He saw the offer as a distraction, and he refocused his attention on his goal. This is how to handle distractions, good or bad. This is how to get things done.

Fifteen years later, he finally got the break he was looking for. His book, *Roots*, was published. It was eventually published in 37 languages, made into a popular television miniseries that broke records for the number of viewers, and won a Pulitzer Prize. Haley became America's *best-selling* African-American author.

Haley was able to stay motivated because he *stayed focused* on a goal that was important to him.

Whatever you have chosen for your goal, you can help yourself stay motivated by staying focused. The focus will make your efforts produce enough progress that you can notice things are moving along. It makes progress clear and obvious. That's *motivating*.

Stay focused on your goal by noticing when you get off track. Notice when you do something that's not related to your important goal, and *stop doing it*. That frees up more time to work toward your goal, which causes you to make more progress per day. Your motivation will intensify as you see the progress.

Use slotras to increase your focus. Repeat things to yourself like, "Stay on track," and "Focus creates power."

Focus Creates Power

We live in a world so rich with possibilities that if you ate a different dish at every meal, you'd never eat them all, and if you watched a different movie every day, you'd never see them all, and if you read a different book every day, you'd never read them all.

In a world like this, it seems awfully foolish to repeat anything — to read the same book twice, or think the same thought over and over again. It *seems* foolish, but it is very much *not* foolish. Repetition can generate power in many different ways and in many different contexts. Let me go over a few to give you an idea.

Obviously the first place to start is with slotras. Repetition is what makes slotras work. Repetition goes over the same pathway in your brain again and again, making that pathway stronger and easier to go down, and that strength and easiness is exactly what makes the slotra worth something. Repeating the slotra allows that thought to be very easy to think, and if it's the right thought for the right context, it can do a lot of good.

That good was created with repetition.

Here's another example of repetition's power: The most *lasting* way to memorize something is a seemingly clumsy, time-consuming, and old-fashioned way: Go over it again and again. If it's a poem, for example, this would mean reciting it again and again. If you go over it enough times, and you will have it memorized. And it will be memorized so well that forty years from now you'll be able to recite it by heart. This is the power of rote learning. *Repetition* generated the power to put something in the mind and have it stick. Repetition has the power to take something as fleeting and insubstantial as a *thought* and make it solid and permanent in the mind.

If you were one of the many children who recited the Pledge of Allegiance to the flag every morning at school, you have with you right now a good example of how solid repetition can make something in an organic organ as soft and alive as the human brain. You can stand up right now, put your hand over your heart and say the whole thing start to finish without batting an eye, and chances are good you haven't said it or even *heard* it for a long time — ten, twenty, maybe even fifty years. But there it is, stable and secure in your mind.

It would seem really old-fashioned to walk by a fifth grade classroom and hear them all chanting aloud the rules of grammar, because that was done in the "olden days." But the rules and facts that were repeated over and over out loud were indelibly imprinted on the mind of those students and never forgotten for as long as they lived.

Unless you're a writer, you probably know very few rules of grammar by heart. I *am* a writer and I hardly remember any of them.

We've gotten away from that sort of learning in our schools, and for some good reasons. But it has its uses for some things, and perhaps we've gotten too far away from it.

One of the arguments against rote learning is that it stifles creativity. But that isn't true. Perhaps *nothing but* rote learning would stifle creativity, but memorizing some things by repeating them over and over doesn't keep the mind from being creative.

Mihaly Csikszentmihalyi, the author of the books, *Creativity* and *Flow*, and a groundbreaking researcher for over forty years, wrote:

> It is a mistake to assume that creativity and rote learning are incompatible. Some of the most original scientists, for instance, have been known to have memorized music, poetry, or historical information extensively.

There's something very calming about well-memorized words. It is a place to come home to, a stable place in a sometimes unstable world of experience. "A person who can remember stories," wrote Mihaly,

> ...poems, lyrics of songs, baseball statistics, chemical formulas, mathematical operations, historical dates, biblical passages, and wise quotations has many advantages over one who has not cultivated such a skill. The consciousness of such a person is independent of the order that may or may not be provided by the

environment. She can always amuse herself, and find meaning in the contents of her mind. While others need external stimulation — television, reading, conversation, or drugs — to keep their minds from drifting into chaos, the person whose memory is stocked with patterns of information is autonomous and self-contained.

Benjamin Franklin wrote in his essay *The Way to Wealth*, "To encourage the Practice of remembering and repeating those wise Sentences, I have sometimes quoted myself with great Gravity."

Of course, he said that tongue-in-cheek, but he *did* create a lot of aphorisms and they *have* been repeated often, and many have become proverbs and rules people live by to this day.

Here are a few of Franklin's gems: Early to bed and early to rise makes a man healthy, wealthy and wise; God helps them that help themselves; Diligence is the mother of good luck; Constant dropping wears away stones; Little strokes fell great oaks, and so on and on. He was fond of making sayings and repeating them often in his writings. He repeated himself so much that others got the ideas stuck in their brains, and they have become a part of our culture.

His rhymes made the aphorisms a little less boring to repeat, but let's face it, repeating anything is boring. But if you will create motivating slotras, or slotras that create a feeling of strength and determination in you, and then practice thinking those thoughts — repeat them to yourself many times every day — you will find a new source of power in accomplishing the goals you want.

Repetition may suck, but it can also suck your goals right into your hands.

That's a good reason to read the same book again rather than a new one. Here's another good reason: Sturgeon's Law. Quoting from Answers.com:

> "Ninety percent of everything is crud." Derived from a quote by science fiction author Theodore Sturgeon, who once said, "Sure, 90% of science fiction is crud. That's because 90% of everything is crud."

When Sturgeon's Law is cited, the final word is almost invariably changed to "crap." Ninety percent of everything is crap. It's got a nice ring to it. And it rings true.

So when you find a good book, *read it again*, or get it as an audiobook and listen to it many times. Why? Because you could read another nine books and you have a good chance of finding that none of them are as good or as useful as the one you've already read and already know is good.

Repetition and Focus

When you need to bolster your courage, when you need to get off your rump and go to work, when you need to overcome your own inertia or nervousness, repeat the following slogan to yourself over and over, making the intensity and urgency of your tone rise each time you say it until it becomes like a war cry — Focus creates power! Focus creates power! Focus creates power!

You'll be up and moving!

In a sense, this is the principle that makes slotras work. By repeating the slogan over and over, you allow your mind to focus, like the sun through a magnifying glass. The sun could shine all day without changing a piece of paper lying on the ground. But use a magnifying glass to focus a lot of light on one little spot, and you'll start to see something happen.

It's like reading a book. You read and get a lot of good ideas, and then get up and go on about your day, and the ideas never had a sharp enough focus onto a single point to make much difference. But take one of those ideas and repeat it and think about it and tell your friends about it, and you'll start to see something happen. Repetition creates focus. Focus creates power.

In experiments on Yoga practitioners, researchers have found that their intense focus during meditation created a specific power: The power to maintain an alpha brain rhythm even during annoying stimulation.

During meditation, the yogis' brain waves slowed down and became rhythmical. It is known as an alpha state, and the state cannot be achieved by force. You can't *make* yourself, by any effort, create that state, because the state of forcing or "making yourself" puts your brain into a beta state, a normal waking state characterized by a faster and more chaotic electrical pulse.

Anyway, once the yogis got into an alpha state, the researchers tried to see what they could do that might jolt them out of alpha and into beta. They tried strong light, a loud banging noise, touching them with something hot, ringing a tuning fork, and sticking their hands into ice-cold water for forty-five minutes. Something they didn't try was smacking them on the back of the head with a baseball bat. I think it would've worked, but I wasn't there at the time and they didn't ask me for my ideas. But anyway, the things they tried didn't work at all. The yogis stayed in alpha, and their alpha rhythm didn't respond at all to any of the annoying stimuli.

By contrast, normal people sitting there who had relaxed enough to be in an alpha state would immediately come out of it from any of those stimuli.

What were the yogis doing? They were simply repeating some stimulus over and over, either saying a word over and over to themselves, or holding a picture in their mind's eye and when they drifted away into other thoughts, bringing it back to that picture or word. Focus is what created the power.

The ability to stay with what you're doing without getting your attention scattered by non-relevant stimuli is a vital component to your general effectiveness in life. Csikszentmihalyi wrote, "If the rock-climber were to worry about his job or his love life as he is hanging by his fingertips over the void, he would soon fall. The musician would hit a wrong note, the chess player would lose the game."

If you can set a goal and stay with it through all the normal distractions of our modern world day after day until you reach your goal, you are in possession of a power to be reckoned with!

Focus creates that power. Even my repetition of this principle in this chapter is creating a certain amount of focus.

But repetition is boring, isn't it? Let's look at that for a moment. Boredom means what? It's an unpleasant state characterized by a wandering mind. Your mind *wanders*, which is the opposite of focus. When you're repeating your slotras, and your mind wanders, you can handle it in one of two ways. I don't know which way is best. Either you can wait until you notice your mind has wandered, and then gently bring it back to repeating the slotra again. That's the peaceful way. If you have too much stress in your life, that's the one I recommend.

If you want more motivation and energy in your life, I recommend the other way: Say your slotra fast enough and intensely enough that your mind doesn't wander very much.

The repetition of the slotra focuses your mental powers on one idea and forms a well-worn pathway through your dendrites (the connections between brain cells).

In Ben Franklin's autobiography, he wrote about how he changed himself. He made a list of thirteen virtues he wanted to acquire, and, he wrote:

> My Intention being to acquire the Habitude of all these Virtues, I judg'd it would be well not

to distract my Attention by attempting the whole at once, but to fix it on one of them at a time, and when I should be Master of that, then to proceed to another, and so on till I should have gone thro' the thirteen...I determined to give a Week's strict Attention to each of the Virtues successively.

His method of concentrating his attention on one at a time worked wonderfully, and through the practice of these virtues, he became one of the most influential men in America during his lifetime.

The most effective formula for success is: Pick one goal and think about it and work toward it all the time. Make it your Magnificent Obsession. There may be many things you want. Earl Nightingale, author of the first spoken audio recording to get a Gold Record (selling a million copies) was an expert on accomplishment. He suggested we write down all our goals, all the things we really want, but then choose *one*. Forget about the others for now.

Choose one and make it your top priority, your most urgent daily obsession. Do this, and keep it up long enough, never giving up, and success is practically *guaranteed*.

Changing Mental Habits

IN THE FAMOUS story of the Uruguayan rugby team that crashed in the Andes mountains, brought vividly to life in the movie, *Alive*, the survivors of the plane crash repeated many phrases — "A man never dies who fights," "We've beaten the cold" — but the one they repeated most often was a simple fact: "To the west is Chile."

Slotralogy is about learning to think thoughts that will help you accomplish your goal. We're talking about the difference between thoughts that occur spontaneously, arising out of the strain of the moment (and are counterproductive) versus thoughts you deliberately design to help you accomplish your goals successfully. That's what the Andes survivors did. Some of their spontaneous thoughts made them despair, of course. But some thoughts gave them strength, and those are the ones the survivors chose to repeat.

You can use the same technique for your goals, whatever they are. Slotras work just as well for the goal of losing weight as they do for the goal of surviving in the Andes.

For best results, take one slotra and work on it diligently for a month or two, practicing your slotra every day. This will form a new habit of thinking that can last a lifetime. Once a habit is formed, it has a certain amount of self-reinforcing momentum of its own. But forming the habit, especially when you already have a *different* habit, takes some regularity.

If you try to change any habit by only practicing it once a week or once a month, it might never change. As you've already learned, that's not often enough. There are too many opportunities during the month to reinforce — to, in effect, *practice* — the old way.

Take one change you want to make and focus on it for a period of time. If you keep trying new things, no habits will form, so no lasting change will take place. That's the bad news: It takes work, discipline, and focus. (If you think you don't have these things, those are the first negative thoughts to change.)

The good news is that if you concentrate, you *can* form new habits.

And during the month or two you're practicing, the practice will keep you thinking the new way as you run across the circumstances your slotras are designed for.

It's like trying to take a new turn on a familiar route. Most people drive to work using the same route every time. If you do that, I'm sure you've had the experience every once in awhile when you're headed in the same direction as your work, but it's a day off and you intend to drive somewhere different. You might need to go about halfway to work, but then turn in a different direction. But what happens? Unless you are paying attention *at the time you need to turn*, you automatically drive toward work. Why? Your brain has formed a habit with repetition.

If you're driving with someone who doesn't work the same place you do, they might immediately say, "Where are you going?"

One of the functions of a slotra is to be like that passenger who notifies you when you start to go the wrong way, the old way. If you practice your slotra every day, you'll have it fresh in your mind, and when you start to think the old way, you will immediately become aware of it. That really speeds up the process of changing a mental habit.

Repetition is the key.

But repetition is redundant. You created the slotra, so you already "know" it, right? But one of the purposes of the repetition is to make sure the new way of thinking is fresh in your mind when it really matters. That's when it counts. "Knowing" it is almost useless.

Insight isn't enough. It is only a first step. The other half is remembering the insight when it matters. That requires repetition.

I suggest you invest money and time in reminders. Draw signs. Create memes to put on your desktop. Make professional posters.

Changing the way you think about something is not a trivial pursuit. You shouldn't do it half-heartedly. It's important. It's worth your time. The way you think determines the quality of your life. This can't be overstated. The way you think determines the quality of your relationships. It determines the amount of money you will make, and how much you manage to keep. It determines how much enjoyment you get out of life. It determines your level of integrity. It determines how well you treat your children and how successfully *they* enter the world.

The content of your mind is the most important thing you have. Invest in making it the best it can be.

Creating a Purpose Slotra

YOUR SLOTRA can be a statement of fact, an idea, a question, or a clear statement of purpose. The effort of trying to create a slotra is *itself* useful — especially when you are creating a statement-of-purpose slotra. The effort to make one will help you clarify your goal. Whatever task you are considering, work out a simple phrase that expresses your purpose. And keep working with it and refining it until you get it down to a simple, clear phrase.

For example, a waiter tries to create one: "I am supposed to take the order and bring the food and drinks." That's only a start. Yes, he's supposed to do those things, but part of his job is his attitude. He could add, "with a good attitude," but it doesn't quite encompass the whole thing, because what about dealing with special requests? What about going beyond the call of duty? What about cooperating and coordinating what he's doing with the busser and the cooks?

He works with it and finally comes up with: "Help them have a good time." This encompasses everything. It helps the customers have a good time if he takes their order — and helps even more if he takes their order when they want it taken. And it helps them have a good time if he brings their food and drink to them — especially if he brings it right after it was made.

And all the little things he does is part of his purpose, beautifully and simply expressed in the phrase, "Help them have a good time." And it's a phrase short enough it can zip through his mind quickly *while he's working*.

And that's why you want your slotras short and sweet. Most tasks require some of your RAM, some of your mental attention, hopefully quite a bit. So if you try to think about your slotra and it is long and difficult to remember, your effort to remember will interfere with what you're trying to do.

Practice saying your statement of purpose when you're not otherwise doing anything important. Repeat it to yourself often. And then when you're actively engaged in a task, think about it once in awhile and make sure you stay on purpose. It'll make your work more efficient. It'll make you more effective. It'll keep you from being sidetracked.

After repeating your purpose-slotra for awhile, the thought will come to you when you need it most. Automatically.

When it does, heed it.

"One of the most dangerous forms of human error," wrote Paul Nitze, "is forgetting what one is trying to achieve."

No matter where you are or what you're doing, this is true: The best use of an idle mind is *thinking about a purpose*. When your mind is cut loose of needing to think about something, it'll tend to eventually think about something unpleasant. There are at least two good reasons for this: First of all, negative stuff is far more compelling than positive stuff. That's the unfortunate truth. How often do you see a crowd gather when a person helps an old lady across the street? But if the old lady gets run over by a bus? That would definitely gather a crowd.

This is not a criticism of the human race. Not at all. It is not a comment on "how low we have sunk." It is nothing like that. We are animals. We have evolved to survive. And part of that is that we have evolved to be acutely aware of danger, and for good reason. Dangerous information turns all our senses on high and compels our attention, even against our will.

Because of that, worries are more compelling than the thought of something nice that might happen, so as your mind wanders around, it won't stick on a nice thought as easily as it will on a scary thought.

But the second reason an aimless mind will gravitate toward negativity is that there are more negative possibilities than positive, so just looking at the numbers alone, the chances are, even if it was purely random, that your mind would think about more negative stuff than positive.

What do I mean there are more negative possibilities? Well, think about health, for example. A positive possibility is that you will be in good health, and for that to be, your spleen has to be functioning right, your knees need to be painless, your teeth need to be cavity-free, and so on. Any one thing wrong and you are not in good health or feeling good.

How many *negative* possibilities do you think there are? As many as the number of things that can go wrong with the human body.

But when you think of good health, it's all one thing, usually. You don't think, "Boy I feel good today. My liver feels good, and my shins feel good. Even my eyelids are doing great!" *It's all one thing*, and so there's not much to think about, except all the million things that could go wrong.

And another reason your mind will be more likely to think negatively when it's idle is that negative things like pain *compel* you to pay attention. In other words, when your elbow hurts, you notice it. You can't help it. The pain draws your attention. But when your elbow is feeling fine, what is there to notice? What would alert your attention to your fine-feeling elbow?

Chances are your elbows have felt fine all day. But until I mentioned it, did you give even one momentary thought to your elbows today?

An idle mind is like a warm damp place where (like bacteria) unhappy thoughts and feelings grow and multiply.

How do you stop your mind from being idle? The best use of an idle mind is thinking about a purpose. If you're actively working on a purpose, there is nothing to worry about, because the purpose and the task at hand will organize your mind and keep your attention too occupied to worry.

But when you're not actively working, when you're driving or waiting in line or taking a shower or lying in bed waiting for sleep, that's when to start thinking about a purpose of yours.

If you have an overriding goal, that's the one to choose. Think about how you're going to get it done. Think about the advantages of accomplishing it. Think about why you want to accomplish it, and think up new reasons. Think about better and more efficient ways of accomplishing the goal. Ponder the goal. Mull it over purposefully. And if you can think of nothing else, use your goal as a slotra and repeat it over and over. This itself, you will notice, brings up new ideas that can help you.

And when you're thinking up good reasons why you want to accomplish this goal and thinking up the advantages you will gain from its accomplishment, *make those into slotras*. Repeat the advantages to yourself.

It is possible to accomplish things without being motivated: Simply make a promise and make sure you keep it. But it is more *fun* to accomplish things when you're motivated. And fun is worth a lot.

One of the best things to focus on when you're driving your car or taking a shower and your mind is wandering aimlessly, is why you are doing what you're doing. *Why* do you want to accomplish your goal? What will it do for you, for your family, for the world at large? And what else? And what else?

It seems strange, but sometimes people set a goal for very good reasons, and then get so busy pursuing it, they actually forget the reasons. And then the purpose begins to feel like you're just going through the motions. It feels like you *have to* do what you're doing. It's not fun any more.

What's the solution for this? One good answer is to keep yourself aware of your motivations by making slotras and practicing them.

Create slotras of your purposes and motivations, and practice thinking those thoughts when your mind is idle. This will keep your mind focused on what you want and prevent negativity from invading your mind. And the process of coming up with good slotras can help you clarify your purposes so you have a better idea of what you really want to accomplish.

The Magic of Motivation

HOUDINI LOVED magic tricks from the time he was a boy, and spent a huge portion of his time learning to amaze people. It was tremendously fun for him. As he started to perform, he didn't make much money. It's a difficult business to succeed at. But he eventually did succeed. He had a motivation he could not forget: The vow he made when he was young to his dying father to financially support his mother for the rest of her life.

He worked unbelievably hard to keep that vow. It was a powerful motivation. His mind was on his purpose every minute of the day.

Consider the patience, persistence, and commitment required to learn just one of the skills he mastered: The ability to swallow something only halfway to the stomach and hold it there, and be able to bring it up again to the mouth.

A Japanese performer showed Houdini the trick, and it took Houdini hundreds of hours of practice to master it, but it enabled him to do his most famous stunts.

He would "swallow" lock-picking tools, but nobody knew this. He dared the finest jails to search him head to toe and lock him up. When he was all locked up, he brought his tools out and escaped from the jail — sometimes making it to the front gate before the jailers did!

Why did he try so hard and work so diligently? Because he had a good *reason*.

Nietzsche said, "He who has a *why* to live for can bear with almost any *how*."

Think about your own *why*. With a good enough reason, you can easily and even joyously bear with any suffering, hardship, difficulty, or tediousness that your goal requires.

And as you're thinking about your reasons, your mind will be electrified with earnest intention and will generate ideas. Eric Hoffer wrote, "We are told that talent creates its own opportunities, but it sometimes seems that intense desire creates not only its own opportunities, but its own talents."

Continually refresh and re-ignite your motivation by thinking about the reasons you really want to accomplish your goal. Make those motivations into slotras (thoughts you practice thinking), and practice thinking them every day.

And thinking about your goals is not the same as *talking* about them. I tend to agree with Earl Nightingale, who certainly knew something about accomplishment. He said:

I've always felt that glibness is a serious danger to accomplishment. Like a steam valve, if we talk at great length about what we are going to do, we seem to lose just that much steam when it comes to actually doing it.

Make statements about your goals and why you want them, and repeat these statements *to yourself*. This is not only positive, it is future-oriented, so it will bring you up, improve your attitude and focus your mind on a definite purposeful action.

When You Backslide

WHEN YOU concentrate on one slotra until you successfully change a thought-habit and then stop practicing your slotra, sometimes you might regress back to your old way of thinking, and the change you accomplished will fade away.

This is not a failure. Please remember this. It is only a regression to old habits. Simply start using the slotra again. The change will come back.

This time, however, keep repeating the slotra even *after* the change is accomplished again, for awhile at least, just to make sure the new mental habit has completely taken hold.

After repeating the slotra for awhile, it will start to come into your mind automatically when you need it. You have successfully changed the way you think, which will change the way you feel and act, which will change the results you get.

This way of dealing with a regression to old habits is a crucially important idea. I can't tell you how many times I've seen people try something, and it works — it improves their lives just as they hoped it would, so they no longer feel they have to worry about it because everything is great, so they stop doing the things that made everything great, which causes things to go back to the way they used to be, and then they conclude, "It didn't work!"

It would be like starting an exercise program and losing fifty pounds and feeling great, and then no longer feeling like you need to exercise because you've been slim now for awhile, so you stop exercising. And then you gain weight. But then, here's the kicker: You conclude that exercise programs don't work.

You probably wouldn't make that kind of mistake with something as obvious as exercise, but you could very easily do it with something as invisible as thought habits, so I am giving you a clear warning which you would do well to heed: Don't make that mistake.

If you find yourself reverting to an old habit, it is because *you stopped doing something*. Start doing what was working before and you will regain your lost benefits.

Talking to Yourself For Fun and Profit

YOU GAIN a lot of benefits by talking to yourself in certain ways. Why do you suppose that is? What is going on? One intriguing theory is that the two separate brain hemispheres in your head function like two different personalities that can influence each other.

This is what we know: The top layer of your brain has two sides, called *hemispheres*, and they function differently. Your left hemisphere, for example, deals with language. Your right hemisphere deals with emotions (I'm oversimplifying here so we can talk about it without going into too much detail).

Research has shown that if the left hemisphere of a man's brain is destroyed by a war injury or stroke, he is unable to speak. He can *feel*. He knows what he *wants* to say, but he doesn't have the brain machinery to put it into words.

If his right hemisphere is destroyed, on the other hand, but his left hemisphere is still intact, he is capable of putting things into words, but he speaks in a monotone: He has no feeling or emotional expression when he speaks.

That is a basic understanding of the brain hemispheres. One side deals with language, reason and logic. The other side processes *emotion* (the brains of women are less compartmentalized than men's but these basic divisions of hemispheric strengths still hold).

Now, if we can extrapolate, we come up with a helpful understanding. The right hemisphere contains emotions, including worries, fears, irrational depressions, and hurt feelings, and if you aren't talking to yourself, that's all there is: A mute emotional brain.

When things are going well, that's great. Emotional feelings of love and happiness are the height of life. But when things are going badly, when you feel negative emotions, it is unpleasant and sometimes more difficult to act in your own best interests.

One of the things I've noticed many times is that when I feel afraid or depressed, my thoughts are a *response* to my feelings. If I feel worried, for example, my thoughts, quite automatically, contain worried images and words. But when I deliberately take over my own thoughts and think what I *want* to think — not at the effect of my feelings, but like a responsible adult talking to an hysterical child — I have noticed that my thoughts can influence my feelings just as much as my feelings influence my thoughts.

So I might say to myself, "Hey wait a minute. It isn't that big of a deal. Even if it turns out badly, it's not a catastrophe. I can do this." This simple, rational self-talk usually calms me down. It makes me saner. More logical. More rational. And my feelings become less negative.

If you've never tried this, I'm sure it must sound too easy. An effective solution can't possibly be that simple. And in a way, that's true. There is a trick to it. Sometimes you have to be firm, as you might with a child throwing a fit. But it doesn't take practice and it isn't difficult. All you have to do is start talking sense to yourself.

Think of it this way: You have two brains. Your right brain is the source of vague worries and fears, which show up as *images* rather than words (imagery is more associated with the right hemisphere). Normally, your left brain picks up the emotional tone and starts adding words like a narrator of a documentary film. Your words embellish the feelings, heightening them and prolonging them.

If you aren't paying attention, if you're just going along with it, you can sink into an unpleasant state of mind in no time at all.

But just turn on your language and see what happens. Take your brain off automatic pilot and start to think what you *want* to think. Say to yourself thoughts you *want* to have going through you mind. Say sane, reasonable, calm, effective things to yourself, and then watch what happens. Your right brain calms down. *You* calm down.

Stop playing the narrator and start directing the film. This is where slotras can save the day. You have practiced them already (when you didn't need them), and now that you could really use some sane thoughts, you have them ready-made.

You can be a *cause* rather than an *effect* of your emotional state. When your feelings are negative, they will naturally alter what you're thinking. You'll automatically think negatively in response to the feelings. But you can turn it around. Think calming thoughts deliberately and your feelings will automatically change in response to your self-talk.

Thoughts Have Consequences

In the book, *In the Heart of the Sea: The Tragedy of the Whaleship Essex*, you can read the fascinating true story of a whaling ship that was deliberately sunk by a whale. This is the event that the fictional story, *Moby Dick*, was based on. It was a whaling ship and they had three small rowboats in the water, chasing after a pod of female sperm whales when a huge male sperm whale, which must have considered the pod his personal harem, saw what was happening and attacked the ship, ramming it head-on twice, sinking it.

After the ship sank, the men in the small boats were left adrift in the middle of the ocean. The three boats were eventually separated, and one of the boats was captained by Owen Chase, who began to give his men coaching in how to think about their circumstances. "I reasoned with them," Chase was later to say, "and told them that we would not die sooner by keeping our hopes."

They had already seen one of their men, Richard Peterson, die, and they all realized that the loss of hope is basically what killed him. Almost as soon as he gave up, he died.

Owen Chase came up with all kinds of arguments and thoughts that would help them stay determined to keep trying and not give up, to keep them from sinking into hopelessness and despair. What he was doing was teaching them how to think about their circumstances — teaching them to think calmly and rationally about their circumstances so their negative feelings wouldn't take over their thoughts and send them to the bottom of the ocean. And it worked.

Another good illustration from the book is about what happens when you feel motivated — what a huge difference it makes. At one point in their long journey in the whaleboats, they were totally laid out, down and out, they could hardly move. They were thirsty, baking in the hot sun, starving, and feeling hopeless.

Suddenly someone sighted land and all of them at once came fully alive! They were up and moving and shouting and rowing with all their might. These were people who were almost dead to the world only a few moments before.

Why? Hopelessness and helplessness suck out the soul, leaving but the shales and husks of men. But the *possibility of success* creates energy and determination.

Consider this: Whether you think something is possible or not is largely in your head, and since confidence in the possibility of success makes such an enormous difference, it is crucial to learn to think in a way that keeps your confidence alive. It is essential to think in a way that keeps you determined and motivated.

Your mental *habits* are the things to master. What electrified the men was the thought that they *might* make it. But think about it: They weren't on land yet. There might not have been any fresh water there. But moments before, most of them were harboring doubt that they would ever make it home alive. That thought is debilitating — maybe as debilitating as severe dehydration or starvation.

That's why it's so important to coach yourself toward confidence and determination and motivation. And coach yourself using slotras — pithy phrases that encapsulate a message.

I don't know about you, but when I first heard about using "positive self-talk" to improve my performance, it didn't strike me as particularly earthshaking. It seems like common sense, doesn't it? Obviously, if you talk to yourself in a confident, reassuring, positive way, you will probably perform most tasks better.

But then it occurred to me, mid-scoff, that as obvious as this seems, *I never did it.* I did not deliberately talk to myself in a confident, reassuring, positive way in order to improve my performance.

So I decided to try the idea on public speaking, a task I was learning to do at the time. And here's what I found: When I thought about an upcoming speech, I'd get a jolt of adrenaline, and that jolt triggered my mind to start thinking a stream of anxious thoughts: "Maybe

I should have picked a better topic. They aren't going to like it. Maybe I can get out of it somehow."

This was a stream of not only anxious thoughts, but anxiety-*provoking* thoughts that made me feel even *more* nervous.

And these thoughts were automatic. I didn't *try* to think these things. They just seemed to happen all by themselves. In fact I tried *not* to think them.

I also found it very easy to take over my own thought-stream. I just interrupted and started talking: "Wait a minute. It is a *good* subject to talk about, and at least some of the people in the audience will be interested. It's going to be okay. I'll do fine. I'll prepare well and when I get up there, I'll just relax and have a good time." This made me feel calmer.

As I already mentioned, I eventually created a slotra that worked better than anything: "I will *make* them get how important this is."

It's *easy* to take over your thoughts and think whatever you want to think. You might not do it naturally, but it is easy.

It's like breathing — when people feel stressed, their breathing *automatically* becomes shallow and high in the chest, and this way of breathing makes them feel more stressed. But once they become aware of it, they can very easily take over their breathing and breathe any way they like.

Self-coaching works the same way. Yes, there may be an automatic thinking style your brain uses when you feel anxious (or any other negative emotion), but you can very easily take over and do it the way you like any time you want. All you need is to be aware of the possibility.

This is good news.

When you want to improve your performance on some task, every time you think about the task, talk to yourself in a confident, reassuring, positive way — especially right before the task. You'll feel better and you'll do better.

And any time you are feeling a negative emotion, deliberately begin talking to yourself calmly, rationally, and logically and your feelings will change in response. Think of it as your left, verbal hemisphere talking to your more emotional right hemisphere.

And if it's a situation that you know is going to repeat itself, you can create and practice good slotras just for that situation.

Your state of mind when doing some things is very important. Before sending their salespeople out to cold canvass, sales managers often talk to their people, pumping them up — trying to get them in the right frame of mind before they start.

Canvassing, or "cold calling," is going out to sell something without an appointment. Starting cold. Just walking in, or knocking on someone's door uninvited, and trying to sell them something. You know how much you dislike being on the receiving end of a cold call, so you can imagine how difficult the job is and how high the rejection level might be. Sometimes it is *worse* than rejection. Sometimes it is hostility.

The sales manager doesn't do anything astonishing to get her salespeople in the right frame of mind. She reminds them of some basic fundamentals: Rejection is part of the process, this is a numbers game, our product is the best they can get at the best price, your job is to turn them on to something good, persistence is the key, and if you are successful, the rewards are high.

By reminding salespeople of these fundamentals *right before* they go do it, their chances of doing well are greater.

Your frame of mind — what's going through your mind — when you do something, and especially when you *begin* something, often has a large influence on how successfully you do it.

With some deliberate effort, you can get yourself in a good frame of mind before doing something you care about, and slotras can help tremendously.

Unremitting Resolution

RELENTLESS resolve can accomplish what seems impossible. In India people called fakirs (which *doesn't* mean they fake anything) do something amazing that takes years to master. They do it as a spiritual discipline. What they choose to do varies.

For example, some hold a particular pose, like a certain religiously appropriate position, and they just keep holding it. This takes intense resolve, because of course, it becomes uncomfortable after only twenty minutes. So they go as long as they can, and then they rest. And then they go as long as they can again, and they keep this up, doing it longer and longer until they are permanently *frozen* in that posture!

They eventually can't move, even if they wanted to. Their disciples have to force feed them and carry them to the river like a statue to wash them off.

This demonstrates the amazing power of unremitting resolution. Personally, I think this *particular* application of will power is stupid. There are so many worthwhile things to accomplish in this world, and these guys have developed their powers of resolve to an unbelievable degree and all they have accomplished is to turn themselves into a statue! I'm sure you can find something better to do with the power of focused resolve.

Robert B. McCall, Ph.D., of the University of Pittsburgh and his colleagues have kept track of 6,700 people for thirteen years. Specifically, they were tracking people who were underachievers in school — people who, according to aptitude tests, had a lot of potential to get good grades, but who, in reality, had low grade-point averages. After thirteen years, only about fifteen percent of them had achieved a career success equal to their abilities.

What did they lack? The two most important things, according to McCall, were: "persistence in the face of challenge," and they were too self-critical. Both of these can be changed. They are both the result of thought-habits.

You are persistent in the face of challenge *if you are in the habit* of being persistent in the face of challenge. And you are in the habit of persisting if you are in the habit of *thinking* in ways that make you persistent.

Get in the habit of telling yourself at key moments, "stay on track." Other good things to tell yourself are "focus creates power" and "do what needs doing" and "every little bit counts."

Persistence is an extremely important habit. You can't really develop competence at anything unless you persist through the rough parts, whether it's playing the piano or doing your job. Any task you undertake, if it's worth your trouble, will have some challenge in it. Some parts of it will be tough. No new abilities can be created without having to persist in the face of challenges, even if the main challenge is suffering through the boring repetition of playing scales on the piano.

For some goals, it will take everything you've got to accomplish it. As a matter of fact, it will take *more* than you've got — you'll have to become more than you are now in order to accomplish it. You'll need to learn more than you now know. You'll need to gain skills you don't have yet.

Practice staying on purpose no matter what distracts you. You will be taken off track again and again until you learn to stick with your purpose. With that kind of focus, you will be a laser beam, cutting through obstacles and barriers with hardly a pause, flying strait to your objective with power and speed.

Summary of Slotralogy

The difference between someone who feels bad and doesn't get much done and someone who feels *good* and gets a *lot* done is simply their mental habits.

The way you think is a habit just like any other habit. When you first learn to drive a car, you really have to pay attention to it. But the more you do it, the more you can do without your conscious attention. *Behaviors* become habits. Whole series of even *complex* behaviors can eventually happen on automatic pilot.

When you drive, your body is on automatic pilot. You pay attention to cars around you, adjust your speed, move the steering wheel so you stay in the center of the lane, adjust your foot to keep your speed just right, and you're doing all this on automatic pilot — by habit — while you carry on a lively conversation with your passenger.

The same is true of your own thoughts. The first few times you think a new thought, you may do it deliberately, but after you've thought a certain way about something over and over several times, it starts to become automatic.

Thoughts influence the way you *perceive* the world. And thoughts alter how you feel. And for the most part, the thoughts you normally think are habit. They aren't deliberate. They're not what you would *choose* if you were choosing your thoughts deliberately.

Change your mental habits and you dramatically change your life.

How? Take a situation where you're having trouble or where you'd like to *feel* or *do* something differently. Now figure out what you want to say to yourself in that situation. What would be helpful to think in that situation? Avoid any statements you don't believe. Try to boil it down into a few short sentences, or even down to one.

Now practice saying that to yourself — in your head, or ideally out loud and with lots of feeling. Say it again and again. Practice thinking that thought. Make it smooth. Make that thought familiar with repetition. Make it come easily to mind by repeating it.

Practice several times a day for awhile so the slotra feels comfortable. Keep practicing until that pathway through your brain seems well-worn. Write the slotra down and carry the paper with you to remind yourself to practice thinking it. Then when the right situation comes up, try to remember to say it to yourself.

It might not work the first time. But after awhile, you'll start to form a new mental habit. Keep practicing, and it will become automatic and you won't have to try to remember any more.

To speed up the process, close your eyes and say your slotra with feeling over and over, and as you do, think about all the different situations in which you would like to think that thought.

Think of the situations, one after the other, where you want that slotra to come to mind, and all the while, repeat it to yourself. This is a way to future-practice, and helps the thought come to mind at the right time. It is also running back and forth on the pathway of your mind, helping to make the slotra easier and easier to think.

To form mental habits to serve you for a lifetime: Create good slotras and practice thinking them until they come to mind automatically.

And never give up.

Never Give Up

IN THE CLASSIC Christmas movie, *It's a Wonderful Life*, the head angel calls an angel-in-training named Clarence and tells him, "A man down on Earth needs our help."

Clarence wants to know, "Is he sick?"

"No. Worse," said the head angel, "he's discouraged."

It *is* worse. Discouragement is like a slow-acting poison that saps our vitality, enthusiasm, and determination. This chapter is an antidote for that poison.

Before we get started, I want you to know I wrote this for both you *and* me. I wrote it for those of us who have heartfelt aspirations that *mean* something to us. I wanted us to have something we could read when we feel like giving up on what we really want to do.

You're going to read about the setbacks and heartaches of great and successful people, and it'll remind us that they doubted themselves at times, and they felt discouraged lots of times, and if we feel that way at the moment, it doesn't mean we're a failure. In fact, it probably means we've got guts enough to try to accomplish something out of the ordinary.

But I have some bad news. In the process of accomplishing your goal, you'll probably experience failure, criticism and ridicule. Some people may even try to stop you. And to top it all off, your goal will probably take longer to accomplish than you think it will.

That's both the bad news and the good news. It's bad news if these things haven't happened to you yet. It's good news if they *have*, because, as you'll be finding out in a minute, people who accomplish extraordinary things usually experience all of these. So if they're happening to you, you're in good company.

As Mickey Rooney once said, "You always pass failure on the way to success."

Milton Hershey went broke twice before succeeding in the candy bar business. The Pepsi Cola company went bankrupt three times. R.H. Macy started a department store that became world famous. But first he went broke *six* times.

You've probably heard of M.A.S.H. — the television series about a medical station in Korea. It was one of the longest running, most popular television programs ever created. But did you know it was turned down by thirty-two different producers? They just didn't think the program would appeal to people.

Robert Pirsig's manuscript for his book *Zen and the Art of Motorcycle Maintenance* was rejected by more than 120 publishers. Seventeen years after its publication it was *still* selling at the rate of a hundred thousand copies a year.

These examples are not unusual. They're the *rule* rather than the exception. People tend to pass failure on the way to success.

Lisa Amos, a professor at Tulane University's School of Business, says that, according to her research, entrepreneurs *average* 3.8 failures before they finally succeed. The same is true for writers, actors, salespeople, painters, and so on. People who succeed, generally speaking, experience failure and rejection and plenty of it.

Slowly But Surely

The first time I ever did the long jump in junior high, I set the school record. I went out for track, thinking success was going to be easy, but then a strange thing happened. Every jump I made after that was shorter and *shorter*. The more I practiced, the shorter my jumps were.

I remember walking home from school one day after practice, a sad and worried little eighth grader, "How could this be happening?" I wondered to myself, "I'm supposed to get *better* the more I practice. Is there something seriously wrong with me?"

I went to a doctor and after a thorough examination, the doctor looked at me solemnly and said, "Son, I'm afraid you've got Osgood-Slaughter's Disease."

"Oh my God!" I was thinking, *"Osgood-Slaughter's Disease!"* I was ready to ask him how long I had left to live when he explained to me it simply meant I was growing very fast and the long jumping was putting a strain on my knees and they weren't able to keep up with the speed of my growth if I kept long jumping. So I took the year off from track, and my knees glued themselves back together.

The next year I went out for track, the coach looked at me and said, "We need a high-hurdler. You're tall and lanky, so you'll be it."

I did the best I could but I was terrible. Sometimes in the junior division I was the only hurdler in the race, and since it was a guaranteed five points, my coach made me run the race by myself. It was so embarrassing. All these people watched while the starter went through the whole ritual. "On your mark...set...POW! And I took off down the middle lane all by myself, awkwardly bounding over the hurdles, smashing into them, knocking them over, and generally making a complete fool of myself as the people in the stands tried not to snicker.

But one thing that usually characterizes the road to success is *perseverance* — to keep at it, to keep learning, and to never give up. The next year I was a little better. I kept studying about nutrition, exercise and muscle growth, and I kept practicing. And a little upon a little, I got better.

As a general rule, goals take longer to accomplish than we think they will. But if we persist, our chances of succeeding keep increasing.

By the end of my senior year of high school I had the school record for the high and low hurdles, and won the CIF Championships for both the high and low hurdles. The CIF is like a state meet for Southern California.

I learned something from that experience that I think is very important. When we first start anything, we're likely to be awkward, uncomfortable, and terrible at it, and people may laugh at us. A lot of times we don't start things because we're afraid we might start out so badly.

Well, I can put that worry to rest right now: You *will* start out badly. It happens to just about everybody when they start on something new. It definitely happened to a boy named Sparky.

In eighth grade, Sparky flunked every single class. He was the worst Physics student in the history of his high school. He also flunked English, Latin, and Algebra.

He went out for the high school golf team. But at the only important match of the year, he lost. There was a consolation match, but he lost that one too.

He was very awkward with people when he was young — sort of a non-human to his classmates. That is, he wasn't either popular *or* unpopular. And in his entire Junior High and High School career, he never went on a single date.

It was clear to everyone that Sparky was a loser.

He thought he was good at drawing, but no one else thought so. In his senior year of high school, he submitted some cartoons for the yearbook, but they were rejected.

He still thought he was good, so he decided to become a professional artist. And he took some action on this goal. He wrote to Walt Disney Studios and they wrote him back, saying, basically, "Make a cartoon out of this subject and send it to us, and we'll take a look at it."

Sparky worked hard on the project. When he was satisfied it was the best he could do, he submitted the material. And then he waited. And waited. And waited some more.

Finally he got a reply from Disney Studios. Sorry Sparky, another rejection.

So Sparky wrote, of all things, an *autobiography!* He made a biography of himself in cartoons. In the cartoons, he called himself Charlie Brown.

Sparky, known to the world as Charles Schultz succeeded beyond his or anyone else's wildest imagination. He *literally* failed himself to success.

What about you? Do you think you have a talent but other people don't think so? The only way to find out who's right is to refuse to give up, to press on and *keep* pressing on, and when you get knocked down by ridicule or rejection, just get back up and keep moving toward your goal.

That's not to say, "Don't listen to anyone." Sometimes even *painful* criticism can be valuable information and can help you achieve your goal. Just don't be *stopped* by it.

Now that's easy to say and harder to do, am I right? I don't know about you, but when someone laughs at my idea or puts me down, sometimes it takes the wind right out of my sails. I start thinking, "Maybe it *is* a stupid idea. Why don't I give it up and quit beating my head against the wall? I haven't got a chance."

The truth is, anyone saying that to himself is probably not going to move ahead very well. Which is why I wrote this chapter.

When you or I feel discouraged, let's re-read this chapter and get some perspective. Let it remind us of the lessons of history. Since the beginning, innovators and achievers and leaders have been ridiculed by the people around them, and it still happens today.

As Eric Fromm wrote, "He who has a conviction strong enough to withstand the opposition of the crowd is the exception rather than the rule, an exception often admired centuries later, mostly laughed at by his contemporaries."

When we get discouraged, let's remember that Marconi's friends (remember Marconi? — inventor of the radio), his own *friends* had him taken into custody and tested in a mental institution. To them, he had obviously lost his marbles since he was going around telling everybody he had discovered a way to send messages through the air without using any wires.

When you and I feel that people don't yet appreciate our worth, let's remember Abraham Lincoln — the greatest president in history in my opinion. Two years before he became president, he went on a lecture tour. It was a miserable failure. In one town, not a *single* person showed up to hear him speak.

While Lincoln was president, the general of his army, George McClelland, once remarked that Lincoln "was nothing more than a well-meaning baboon."

In 1863, in a commentary in *The Chicago Times*, the Gettysburg Address was severely criticized. *The Gettys-*

burg Address! One of the most eloquent speeches ever delivered. It was summed up as "silly, flat, and dishwatery utterances."

We recognize great contributions in retrospect, but often, at the time, people don't understand it. They don't see it. Or they're envious.

John Adams once called George Washington "an old muttonhead." He said Washington was "too illiterate, unread, and unlearned for his station and reputation."

The Experts Might Be Wrong

When you get criticized, remember that when Ludwig van Beethoven was being taught music, his composition teacher said — no doubt with a tone of complete authority — that Beethoven was a hopeless dunce.

When Marilyn Monroe's contract elapsed in 1949, Columbia Pictures did not extend it or make a new one. Why? Because producer Harry Cohen thought Marilyn Monroe "lacked star quality."

Gilda Radner, one of the original cast of Saturday Night Live, once did a show called "Gilda Live." When it opened in Boston, the newspaper had a review with this headline, "Gilda Radner has no talent. Zip. Zilch. Zero."

Lucille Ball was on the chorus line of a road company when she was fired and told, "You're not meant for show business. Go home."

The first reviews of Hans Christian Anderson's fairy tales said, "Quite unsuitable for children. Positively harmful for the mind."

When Ronald Reagan tried out for the leading role in a film called *The Best Man* in 1964 (before he was a politician) he was rejected because, "he doesn't look like a president." Is that ironic or what?

Rudyard Kipling had already written what is now considered one of the best short stories ever written — *The Man Who Would Be King* — when he was fired from his job as a reporter for the *San Francisco Examiner*. His boss said, "I'm sorry Mr. Kipling, but you just don't know how to use the English language. This isn't a kindergarten for amateur writers."

When Albert Einstein was in school, his Greek teacher told him, "You will never amount to anything."

Napoleon Bonaparte once listened to Robert Fulton, the inventor of the steamship, and when he couldn't stand it any more, he interrupted Fulton, "What sir?! You would make a ship sail by lighting a bonfire under her decks? I pray you excuse me. I have no time for such nonsense."

Fulton wasn't fazed a bit. By that time he was used to people telling him it wasn't possible. In fact, the whole time he was building his steamship he didn't hear a *single* encouraging remark. People made fun of him and his crazy idea.

It turns out that steam power revolutionized the shipping industry.

Winston Churchill was a rebellious youngster, and in school he did poorly in every subject except history.

He *hated* school. He was late for class repeatedly. Different teachers at different times wrote the following descriptions of him on their school reports:

> careless
> a regular pickle
> very naughty
> troublesome
> very bad
> a constant trouble to everybody

Robin Williams was criticized by his elocution teacher in college. The teacher said to Williams, "You're *mimicking* people. Where is *your* voice?" His claim to fame, his amazing ability to imitate voices, was criticized. There he was, a nobody, a college kid, and "The Expert" is telling him that what he's doing is wrong and he should change. He should become more like everyone else.

WARNING WARNING: *This is subversive material you're reading here.* I'm encouraging you to be a nonconformist. I'm encouraging you to go against the tidal wave of forces that want you to be anybody but yourself.

Generally speaking, people don't want you to be what you are. They would rather you were more like what *they* want you to be. People want you to become "well adjusted," which means you should adjust to *their* values and biases.

But, as Earl Nightingale said, "Advances don't come from happy, well-adjusted, well-integrated people. They come from non-conformists who refuse to buy the status quo."

J. Paul Getty, who was *the richest man in the world* when he died, said, "There are many pressures that try to force the young person of today to be a conformist. He is bombarded from all sides with arguments that he must tailor himself, literally and figuratively, to fit the current image, which means that he must be just like everyone else. He does not understand that the arguments are those of the almost-were's and the never-will-be's who want him as company to share the misery of their frustrations and failures."

As Herbert Bayard Swope said, "I cannot give you the formula for success, but I can give you the formula for failure: try to please everybody."

Ferdinand Oliver was a woman who lived with Picasso for seven years. The whole time they were together, they lived in poverty. She didn't like Picasso's paintings. She especially didn't like the paintings he did of *her*. She thought they made her look ugly.

In 1912, after seven years of squalor, she moved out and never saw Picasso again. In 1966 she died, still in poverty. A few years later, one of those unflattering paintings of her by Picasso sold for $790,000.

Now what if Picasso had said, "All right Ferdinand, I'll paint it right," and then painted a picture to please her, a picture she would consider flattering? If he had tried to please her, we never would have *heard* of him. His greatness was in following his own way. He went against the forces that would make him be like everyone else.

If there's a certain thing you want to do — like Picasso, who wanted to make a certain kind of painting — and people tell you, "It's no good, it'll never work, it's a crazy idea, why don't you knock it off and do something productive, just say, as Edward R. Murrow used to say, "You may be right," and continue doing what you want to do. If you think you have talent and some person, even an expert, comes along and tells you you're no good, pursue your talent anyway, because they just may be dead wrong.

At age 18, Anita Baker almost gave up on her goal of being a singer when a record executive, after he had listened to her sing, told her bluntly, "Anita, you have no talent."

Even the late Jack LaLanne, a man respected and admired all over the world, had a hard time at first. When he opened a fitness club, people thought he was out of his mind. Really! His was the very first fitness club ever opened in the US.

He was trying to convince people that exercise was a good idea. What a nut, huh? He was labeled a charlatan and a quack. But he would not give up. He himself was thoroughly convinced of the benefits of exercise. So he built a gym in his backyard and started working out. After awhile, other people wanted to use it, so he let them. Then he started charging a fee for people to come use it, and eventually he opened a fitness club.

At the time, doctors actually *warned* their patients *not* to go to Jack LaLanne's club. "You'll get a heart-attack," they said, "You'll get hemorrhoids. You'll lose your sex drive. If you're an athlete, you won't be able to throw the ball."

He wasn't stopped by these criticisms. He was a non-conformist. He followed his own way and pioneered our present respect for exercise. And he was proof that the old status quo was wrong and needed to be changed. At 77 years old he was breaking records he set when he was 21.

Speaking of health, have you ever heard of a man named Paracelsus? He did a very good thing for you and me. In the year 1500 AD, the doctors in Europe studied the work of a man named Galen, whose works had been respected for 1300 years. That's an incredibly long time. You talk about well established! What he wrote became like sacred doctrine. If Galen wrote it, it was so, and that's all there was to say about it.

Now a lot of the things he wrote were accurate. But a lot of it was garbage. For example, supposedly inside each person were what were called the Four Cardinal Humors. Humor comes from the Latin *umor* meaning fluid or moisture.

The four Humors were Phlegm, Choler, Blood, and Melancholy. In order to be in good health, so the theory went, a person had to have a proper balance between these humors. The whole thing sounds pretty humorous, don't you think? But if you didn't have enough of one of these humors, or if you had too much of one, then you were sick. That's what disease was. So to make you well, the doctor's job was to restore the balance.

Galen also believed that each person had a certain balance that was just right for that particular individual. Therefore, each illness *in each person* was unique.

So the doctor, with his special knowledge, might find you had, say, too much of one of your humors, blood for example. And he would treat you by making you bleed for awhile. One of their techniques was to attach leeches to your body to suck out some of your blood. And then you would be well.

Now this sounds like a good Monty Python gag, but here were *well-respected authorities*, diligently studying for *years* to get their "Doctor of Physic" degree so they could go out and make people sweat and purge and bleed and vomit, and thereby supposedly make them healthy. A lot of the time, as you can probably imagine, the treatment *killed* the patient. But after 1300 years, this was a very well-established status quo.

Then along comes a rebel by the name of Paracelsus, who came up with the scandalous idea that something from *outside* your body, like smoke or germs, could make you sick. What a radical! He was viciously attacked by the medical profession, so he never stayed in one place very long, and he lived his life in poverty.

But he never gave up. He felt pretty sure he was right, and he knew if he *was* right, it would have an enormous impact on the health of everyone.

Since he had no Doctor of Physic degree, he was never allowed to publish his ideas — including his studies on the many people who worked in mines who all seemed to die of the same thing (now called Miner's Disease) which would seriously put in question one of Galen's "sacred" ideas that all diseases were unique.

It wasn't until a couple of decades *after* Paracelsus died that his work became known and published. He turned out to have been right, and although he never knew what he did, he opened up the way for a whole new approach toward disease, and doctors dramatically increased their effectiveness because of that persistent rebel.

Now some people might consider themselves a failure if they lived a life like Paracelsus — in poverty and scorned by his peers. But there are more important things in life than just winning or getting everyone's admiration, or collecting and spending a lot of money. Nothing *wrong* with these things. Not at all. But there's at least one thing that's more important: Being true to your own aspiration.

If it stirs you, if that vision captivates you, if the ideas for that invention haunt you and won't leave you alone, if you have a goal that may even seem petty to others, but it's something you feel is good and right, and you want to try...then do it, no matter how long it takes or who thinks you're a fool. Never give up on something that matters to you.

Go ahead and give up on other things, but never let your dream die.

Did I say go ahead and give up on some things? Hey! What's going on here? In a chapter called *Never Give Up* I'm saying go ahead and give up?

You bet. As Joshua Leebman wrote, "Every person who wishes to attain peace of mind must learn the art of renouncing many things in order to possess other things more fully."

Or as Dr. Michael Broder put it, "You can have practically anything you want, but not everything you want."

I've never met anyone who doesn't want more than they have time to pursue. There's an important principle in writing and public speaking that translates well into life: Cut out the unimportant and the important becomes clearer and better.

Most people don't live so simply. There are a lot of people trying to "have it all," and even more who have completely given up on, or forgotten, the goal that really means something to them. And one of the ways we human beings know how to behave and what to do is by looking around and seeing what *other* people are doing. You won't see many people trying to renounce some things in order to possess their dream more fully.

So when people see what you're doing, they will probably have something to say about it. *They will comment on your life.*

Family Support

If you do something remarkable, people will remark about it — especially your family — and most of them will have only negative things to say. As William Thackeray put it, "If a man's character is to be abused, there's nobody like a relative to do the business."

When Winston Churchill was young, his father concluded that Winston was "Unfit for a career in law or politics" because he did so badly in school.

Barbra Streisand's mother told her directly that she wasn't pretty enough to be an actress and she would *never* become a singer because her voice wasn't good enough.

Conrad Hilton, who created a business empire with his Hilton Hotels, once overheard his father say to his mother, "Mary, I do not know what will become of Connie. I'm afraid he'll never amount to anything."

When Charles Darwin wanted to go on his five year expedition on the Beagle — the voyage that began his rise to fame and secured his name in the highest rank of scientific achievement, his father was against the whole idea. All he could see was that his son was drifting into life of "sin and idleness."

How many discoveries and accomplishments have never been realized because so many people listen to the criticisms of their relatives? The Native American tribe, the Osage, had a saying that if you want a place in the sun, you'll have to leave the shade of the family tree.

When Arnold Schwarzenegger discovered weight lifting, he started working out two hours before school and two hours after school every day. His parents thought he was out of his mind. Arnold wanted to be the best built man in the world, and then he planned on going to America to be in movies.

When his parents found out that was his goal, they seriously talked about sending him to a psychiatrist.

How was he able to keep going even as a young man in the face of the opposition from his parents? One time when he was fifteen years old he'd had a particularly grueling workout, and at the breakfast table the next morning he was so stiff and sore, that when he tried to take a drink of his coffee, he spilled it all over the table.

His mother came over to the table and looked at him. "What's wrong Arnold? What is it?"

"I'm just sore," he said, "my muscles are stiff."

She yelled out to Arnold's father, "Look at this boy! Look what he's doing to himself!"

In his biography, after relating this incident, Arnold makes a comment that reveals the attitude that allowed him to continue in the face of his parents' opposition. He wrote, "I couldn't be bothered with what my mother felt."

He was so intent upon his purpose, he just *couldn't be bothered* with it. He didn't fight it, he didn't try to change her opinion. He simply went about his purpose. A lot of people would have stopped what they were doing to try to make their mother happy. That's one way aspirations die.

George Washington's mother was a harping, complaining, self-centered woman by all accounts. She put down Washington's accomplishments, and didn't show up to either of his presidential inauguration ceremonies. She was always whining when her children neglected her, and she was especially enraged when her son George ran off to command the army for the American Revolution! She honestly believed *it was George's duty* to stay home and take care of his mother.

I'm sure glad *he* didn't think that was his duty.

In the sixteenth century there was a young man named Tycho Brahe. His parents had money, and sent him off to a prestigious school to study law, but he wasn't interested in law. The love of his life was observational astronomy. The only problem was, there was no such subject as observational astronomy.

So he studied law during the day to keep his parents happy, but at night he went out and watched the movements of the stars and planets, and he kept records of these observations.

It was the records that eventually made a difference in the history of science. But his parents didn't like him wasting his time stargazing, and insisted he concentrate on his law studies. They hired a tutor to keep him focused. But while his tutor slept, Tycho Brahe was out observing the stars.

Had he obeyed his parents, history would have been different. But he followed his own star, so to speak, and eventually found himself teaching others his methods and findings. Among these students was Johannes Kepler, who studied Tycho Brahe's huge collection of recorded observations, and then, based on these, created the Three Laws of Planetary Motion, which brought into being *an entirely new science*: Physics.

And all this came about because Tycho Brahe followed that deep impulse, against the wishes of his well-meaning parents.

There's a moral to these stories. Don't try too hard to please your parents. They have goals for you that may not match *your* goals for you, and it's *your* goals that must be satisfied by *your* actions. If your parents have goals, it's *their* job to accomplish them, not yours. Your job is to achieve your own goals.

In his youth, Leonard Bernstein, one of the most talented and successful musicians in American history, was continually pressured by his father to give up his music and do something worthwhile, like help out in his family's beauty-supply business. In Bernstein's early days, his father was disappointed that his son was so interested in music.

After his son became famous, the father was asked about that, and he said, "Well how was I supposed to know he was *the* Leonard Bernstein?"

Let this be a lesson to us, both as parents and as children. If you're a parent, your child might be *the* Leonard Bernstein, or *the* Picasso, or *the* Tycho Brahe, and if you're a child, and you have a goal your parents don't support, take heart! They don't know that you are who you are, and they *won't* know until you've done it.

Most of us want our parents to approve of what we're doing. But disappointing them, at least for awhile, might be something you'll have to live with. Sometimes they don't want you to pursue your goal because it's risky and they don't want to see you suffer failure. And since *you* don't want to fail either, their arguments against your goal can be very persuasive, because failure is, apparently, the *worst* thing that could happen.

But maybe it would actually be worse to not even try. "Many people die," said Oliver Wendell Holmes, "with their music still in them." That's tragic.

Failure is a possibility. No doubt about it. And it wouldn't do much good to ignore it. Maybe your manuscript will get sent back. Maybe you won't get the job. Maybe your idea will be a flop. Maybe the thing you fear will actually happen. Since, when we begin anything that requires any skill or creativity at all, we're going to be making mistakes right and left, the only road to accomplishing our goal is through making mistakes, is through failing. What a bummer, right? But not really. Because after awhile you get over the *bummer* of making mistakes, and you begin to see the value that's there.

As Ralph Waldo Emerson wrote, "Bad times have a scientific value. These are occasions a good learner wouldn't miss."

Or as Francois Duc de la Rochefoucauld wrote, "There are no circumstances, no matter how unfortunate, that clever people do not extract some advantage from, and none, no matter how fortunate, that the unwise cannot turn to their own disadvantage."

Failure and Success

"When I was young," said George Bernard Shaw, "I observed that nine out of ten things I did were failures. So I did ten times more work."

Winston Churchill said, "Success is going from failure to failure with great enthusiasm."

Buckminster Fuller said that parents kill off the genius of their children *by making them afraid* of making mistakes.

When you're afraid of making mistakes, you initiate fewer actions, and when you initiate fewer actions you don't *fail* as much, but you also don't *learn* as much. Being afraid of making mistakes prevents you from becoming as good as you could be. That must be why Thomas Watson said, "The way to succeed is to double your failure rate."

Watson was working for a company called National Cash Register, otherwise known as NCR, when he was fired. But he vowed that he would develop a company that would *dwarf* NCR some day. He went on to create a company called International Business Machines, otherwise known as IBM.

Watson once gave some advice to a writer who was discouraged because so many publishers had rejected his manuscripts. Watson told him, "You're making a common mistake. You're thinking of failure as the enemy of success. Every one of those manuscripts was rejected for a reason. Have you pulled them to pieces looking for a reason? You've got to put failure to work for you. Go ahead and make mistakes. Make all you can. Because remember, that's where you'll find success — on the far side of failure."

"Fear nothing," said Katherine Tingley, "for every renewed effort raises all former failures into lessons, all sins into experience." Every time you pick yourself up and try again, you transform your failure into a lesson. Remember that quote as you read the story of a man who wanted very much to be an actor.

The man was turned down by *hundreds* of agents. Now, rejection has got to be one of the hardest things in the world to take. But he took it, one day at a time, and although it hurt, he didn't let it stop him.

Nobody wanted him as an actor, so he bought a book on how to write a screenplay and wrote his own movie. His plan was to sell a package deal: You want the screenplay? I'll sell it to you if I get to play the leading role. But again, nobody was interested. He was rejected again and again, but he kept at it.

Then a company made him an offer just when he desperately needed money. His wife was pregnant, and they had less than a hundred dollars to their names. He was offered *two hundred and sixty five thousand* dollars for the script...on one condition: That *he* wouldn't star in it. They wanted someone like Burt Reynolds or Warren Beatty.

But he wrote it, and he thought his movie would make him a star — but only if he starred in it. So he bit the bullet and refused to sell out.

Boy, that must have been tough. And you know, no matter what your goal is, it will probably be tough. It's important that you make up your mind to be willing to sacrifice some comfort for the sake of your goal, because it *will* be necessary for your goal's achievement.

An interviewer once asked Ray Bradbury about the sacrifices he made early in his career. "Wasn't it hard to make sacrifices? Didn't you have to give up most of the things people feel they have to have?"

Bradbury said, "Well, it depends on what you have to have. You can get along on a very small amount of money." Then he talked about not going to the theater, giving up movies, not buying clothes, and eating lots of macaroni and cheese and cans of soup.

You know what kills a lot of aspirations? *Impatience.* People don't want to sacrifice the nice car and the stylish clothes and the great iPhones and all those other luxuries that seem like necessities, so they buy them, and then they're in debt, so they don't have the freedom to do what they want. They don't have any money to finance their goal, so the goal gets shoved aside. After awhile, they forget it's even there.

Big obstacles didn't kill the dream. Impatience did.

A friend of mine told me the other day she's tired of the fashion industry and she wants to do something meaningful with her life, but she doesn't know what that would be.

"If money wasn't an issue," I asked her, "what would you love to do?"

Oh!" she said immediately, "I've always wanted to work with troubled kids."

"Well there's your answer," I said, "How about getting out of the fashion industry and working with troubled kids?"

She looked at me as if I was unbelievably naive. "There's no money in it," she said. And with that simple statement, she slammed the door on something that may have made her life satisfying.

She has charged so much money for clothes on her credit cards, she couldn't realistically get into another line of work that pays less for at least a couple of years. It would take that long to pay off the cards.

That would be hard. She could do it. But it would be hard.

Being willing to sacrifice, being willing to delay gratification, *gives you power.* We may not *like* driving the old car. We may *prefer* to have all the nice things everyone else has. And if we sacrifice and keep pursuing our goals, we'll probably be able to have those nice things. But for sure we'll have something that's way more valuable: We'll be satisfied with our life.

So what happened to our would-be actor and screenwriter? The company offered him $265,000 but he refused because he wanted the leading role. He went back to knocking on doors and finally a company took a risk on his movie *and* his acting. But they tried to lower their risk by paying him only a little bit up front and then ten percent of the profits.

The movie was *Rocky* and it won academy awards for best director and best picture and made an unknown man named Sylvester Stallone into a star. Seven other *Rocky* films were made, grossing more than a *billion* dollars.

Stallone, the actor and screenwriter, had the courage to keep trying. There are millions of people who would *like* to succeed but very few of us are willing to suffer and sacrifice and keep going because it's tough, it's discouraging and to keep going we need that rare and precious quality: Perseverance. As Samuel Johnson said, "Great works are performed, not by strength, but by perseverance. He that shall walk, with vigor, three hours a day, will pass, in seven years, the circumference of the globe."

Perseverance

Case in point: John Johnson, the richest African American in the United States, publisher of *Ebony* and *Jet* magazines, owner of a multimillion dollar cosmetics and insurance empire, and a man with formidable perseverance.

He started out dirt-poor, barefoot, and living in a tin-roofed shack in the deep South. His first publishing venture, when he was just twenty-four years old, was a little magazine called *Negro Digest*. He went to get a loan to start his business, and they laughed in his face. The assistant to the assistant was the only person he could talk to at the bank and he told Johnson, "Boy, we don't make any loans to colored people."

No banks were willing to invest any money in his enterprise, so his mom let him put her furniture up for collateral on a $500 loan. He wanted the African Americans in the South to read his magazine because a lot of them thought they were inferior people. They had been oppressed for generations. They needed to be inspired, and Johnson knew his *Negro Digest* would do that.

The problem was that the police in the South were hostile to black-oriented media. So Johnson got clever. He had his agents board buses and secretly sell the *Digest*, working from seat to seat to the next stop.

Some of these agents were caught, beaten, and jailed. But they kept at it, and *Negro Digest* became a success.

When Johnson started *Ebony Magazine*, he had a hard time getting companies to advertise in it because nobody wanted their advertisements in a magazine for African Americans. He sent letters and made phone calls. He personally made 400 phone calls to a single CEO.

The car industry was the hardest. As Johnson said, "We sent an advertising salesman to Detroit every week for *ten years* before we broke our first major account." Now that's perseverance!

John Johnson got his accounts, kept his magazines going, and inspired millions of people in the process.

Perseverance isn't a single, massive effort. It's constant effort over a long period of time. For example, in the *Guinness Book of World Records*, there's a man who ate a bicycle. Yep, swallowed a whole bicycle.

If you think about doing that yourself, it sounds pretty difficult, doesn't it? And when you and I hear about the successes of others, and we think about doing it ourselves, it sounds pretty difficult too. But if you watched the bicycle-eater perform his seeming miracle, you would recognize that you could do the same thing...if you wanted to.

And that's also likely true about the successful people we know about. If we followed them around night and day, week after week, after awhile we would realize that *we* could accomplish the same thing if we wanted to.

The secret of the successful people *and* the bicycle-eater is to *do what you can for today*, and keep it up most every day.

The bike-eater had the entire bicycle ground into a fine powder, and every day he added a little of this powder to his meals. It took him awhile, but he eventually ate the whole bicycle. Pretty easy. Yes. And that's the point. There may be things along the way that are difficult to stomach. I'm sure it wasn't easy for John Johnson to be rejected so many times. But he didn't try to get *every* company to advertise in one day. And the bicycle-eater didn't try to swallow a whole bike's worth of powder in one day. It would have killed him.

They did what they could each day, and kept doing that most every day for a long time. By the way, I told a little fib. The guy who ate the bicycle didn't really eat *a* bicycle. He ate *ten* bicycles. His name was Michel Lotito. He ate ten bikes, a supermarket cart, seven TV sets, six chandeliers, and a low-calorie Cessna light aircraft.

A little every day adds up to a lot.

We just need to do a *little* today, and again tomorrow. The effect will accumulate. Sometimes what we do will be successful, and sometimes we'll make mistakes. But as the Japanese proverb says, the secret of success is "Fall seven times, stand up eight." That's what Jimmy Yen did. He isn't Japanese, he's Chinese, and you've probably never heard of him. Most Westerners haven't. But a jury of distinguished scholars and scientists, including Albert Einstein and one of the Wright brothers (Orville), thought enough of him to vote him one of the top ten "modern revolutionaries" of the twentieth century.

What did Jimmy Yen do that was so astounding? He taught Chinese peasants to read. Big deal, right? But for four thousand years, right up through the 20th century, reading and writing in China was only done by the scholars, and was considered beyond the ability of the peasants. "Everybody knew," including the peasants themselves, that peasants were incapable of learning.

That belief, that *thoroughly ingrained*, four thousand year-old belief, was Jimmy Yen's first so-called "impossible" barrier. The second barrier was the Chinese language itself, consisting of 40,000 characters, each character signifying a different word. The third barrier was the lack of technology — even the lack of good roads. How could Jimmy Yen even *reach* the 350 million peasants in China?

Impossible odds. An impossibly huge goal. And yet he had almost attained it when he was forced, by Communism, to leave his country. Did he give up? No. He decided to teach the rest of the developing world to read! Practical reading programs, like the ones he'd developed in China started pumping out literate people like a gushing oil well in the Philippines, Thailand, Sri Lanka, Nepal, Kenya, Columbia, Guatemala, Indonesia, Bangladesh, Ghana, India — *people became literate.* For the first time in their entire genetic history, they had access to the accumulated knowledge of the human race.

For those of us who take literacy for granted, I'd like you to consider for a moment how narrow your world would be if you'd never learned how to read, and there was no access to radios, the internet, or TVs.

Chinese peasants were hired by the Allied Forces in World War One, as laborers in the war effort, 180,000 of them. Most of them had no idea — not a clue — where England, Germany or France was. They didn't know what they were being hired to do. And they didn't even know what a *war* was! Try to grasp, if you can, the vacancy, the darkness, the *lack* that existed in those people because they couldn't read. Jimmy Yen was a *savior* to them.

At one point he published a little newspaper for the Chinese peasants working there in Europe, where he started his literacy program, when he received a letter from one of his former students. The student wrote:

> "Ever since the publishing of your paper, I began to know everything under the heavens. But your paper is so cheap, and costs only one centime a copy, you may have to close your paper down soon. So here please find enclosed 365 Franks which I have saved during my three years labor in France."

Now get this: The Chinese peasants in France were being paid *one Frank a day* — the equivalent of twenty cents. And this poor laborer sent his entire savings, *more than a year's pay*, to Jimmy Yen!

How much would something have to mean to *you* for you to voluntarily, happily, give away more than a year's worth of your income out of sheer gratitude?

What was the secret of Jimmy Yen's success? He found a real need and he found in himself a strong desire to answer that need. And he took some action. He tried to do something about it, even though it seemed impossible. He worked long hours. He started with what he had in front of him, and he gradually took on more and more.

Thomas Carlyle said, "Our main business is not to see what lies dimly in the distance, but to do what lies clearly at hand."

And that's what Jimmy Yen did. He started out teaching a few peasants to read. He had no desks, no pens, no money, no overhead projectors. He started from where he found himself and did what was clearly at hand.

Each time a new class started, there were more people in it, and he got better and better at teaching them. And as time went on, he received more and more help.

Opportunities

What's clearly at hand for you? Do *you* have a tendency to dream big, to try to figure out in advance what lies dimly in the distance, ignoring the opportunities for a small beginning right here, right now?

"Nobody has made a greater mistake," wrote Edmund Burke, "than he who did nothing because he could only do a little."

Everyone has heard of Mother Teresa. But do you know how she *began* her mission? She started by simply doing the little task that lay clearly at hand. She was a twenty-one year old teacher at a convent high school in Calcutta, India, looking out her window one day at the slum on the other side of the concrete wall. This wasn't the kind of slum you and I normally think of, though. This was a slum that would make the poorest of poor Americans shudder. Open sewers, rampant disease, widespread famine — it was *horrible*.

After school, Sister Teresa went into the slum and brought those people medicine and bandages. She did *what she could* from where she was *with what she had*. She discovered her mission: To help the poor while living among them. She left the area to get a little more education, then came back to the slum and went to work.

The kids needed to learn to read and write, because without those essentials, they could never rise above their condition. But she had no resources. So she wrote letters in the dirt with a stick, with at first only five or six children. That was her school. The dirt on the ground. A stick. And a few children.

But of course the parents of the children saw what was happening, so pretty soon some tables appeared. Then eventually benches and a blackboard. As word got around, more and more children were showing up for class.

She *saw a need*, and she tried to fill that need directly, doing what she could with what she had, a little on a little, no matter how small it seemed, and by following that simple strategy, she became a world leader of sorts, an inspiration to millions of people, and in 1979, received the Nobel Peace Prize.

What's your mission? You can dream as big as you want to dream. Just realize that you can only do something about it *today*. Yesterday is already gone, and tomorrow isn't here yet. So everything you'll ever accomplish, no matter how big, will be accomplished one day at a time. So go ahead and get in your mind whatever it is you really want. But then bring it down to a focus by asking yourself, "What can I do *this* day to advance toward my dream?" Now do that. Today. No matter how hopelessly impossible the big goal seems to be, no matter who thinks it's a silly idea, no matter how many times your idea has been rejected, take one step forward on it today.

This is the Path of Progress, and the Way to Happiness. It's the way to the achievement of your mightiest aspirations. It's the way Sylvester Stallone and Mother Teresa and Jack LaLanne and every achiever accomplishes their goals. And it's also the way Paul Rokich achieved his goal.

When Paul was a boy growing up in Utah, he happened to live near an old copper smelter, and the sulfur dioxide that poured out of that refinery had made a desolate wasteland out of what used to be a beautiful forest.

When a young visitor one day looked at this wasteland and saw that there was nothing living there — no animals, no trees, no bushes, no birds, no anything but fourteen thousand acres of black and barren land that even *smelled* bad — this kid looked at the land and said, "This place is crummy."

Paul knocked him down. He felt insulted. But he looked around, and something happened. Paul Rokich, in that moment, made a vow that someday he would bring back the life to this land.

Many years later, Paul was in the area, and he went to the smelter office. He asked if they had any plans to bring the trees back. *No* was the answer. He asked if they would let *him* try to bring the trees back. *No.* They didn't want him on their land.

He realized he needed to be a lot more knowledgeable before anyone would listen to him, so he went to college to study botany. At the college, he met a very inspiring professor who was an expert in Utah's ecology.

Unfortunately, this expert told Paul that the wasteland he wanted to bring back was beyond hope. He was told that his goal was foolish because even if he planted trees there, and even if they grew, the wind would only blow the seeds forty feet per year, and that's all you'd get because there weren't any birds or squirrels to spread the seeds, and the seeds from *those* trees would need *another* thirty years before they started producing seeds of their own.

Therefore, it would take approximately 20,000 years to revegetate that six-square-mile piece of earth. His teachers told him it would be a waste of his life to try to do it. It just plain could not be done.

So he tried to go on with his life. He got a job operating heavy equipment, got married, had some kids...but his dream would not die. He kept reading up on it, and he kept thinking about it. And then one night he took some action. He did what he could with what he had.

This was an important turning point. As Samuel Johnson said, "It is common to overlook what is near by keeping the eye fixed on something remote. In the same manner," he said, "present opportunities are neglected, and attainable good is slighted, by minds busied in extensive ranges."

Paul stopped busying his mind in extensive ranges and looked at what opportunities for attainable good were right in front of him. Under the cover of darkness, he sneaked out into the wasteland with a backpack full of seedlings, and started planting. For seven hours, he planted seedlings.

He did it again a week later. And every week, he made his secret journey into the wasteland and planted trees and shrubs and grass. But most of it died.

For *fifteen years* he did this.

Freezing winds and blistering heat, floods and landslides and fires destroyed his work time and time again. But he kept planting.

One night he found a highway crew had come and taken tons of dirt for a road grade, and all the plants he had painstakingly planted in that area were gone. But he just kept planting.

Week after week, year after year, he kept at it — against the opinion of the authorities, against the trespassing laws, against the devastation of road crews, against the wind and rain and heat, even against plain common sense — he just kept planting.

Slowly, *very* slowly, things began to take root. Then gophers appeared. Then rabbits. Then porcupines. The old copper smelter at first gave him permission, and then later (as times were changing and there was political pressure to clean up the environment) the company eventually *hired* Paul to do what he was already doing, and they provided him with machinery and crews to work with. Progress accelerated.

Now the place is fourteen thousand acres of trees and grass and bushes, rich with elk and eagles. And Paul Rokich has received almost every environmental award Utah has.

He says, "I thought if I got this started, when I was dead and gone people could come and see it. I never thought I'd live to see it myself."

It took him until his hair turned white, but he managed to keep that "impossible" vow he made to himself as a child.

Now, what was it *you* wanted to do you thought was impossible? Sure gives a perspective on things, doesn't it?

The way you get something accomplished in this world is to just keep planting. Just keep working. Just keep plugging away at it, one day at a time for a long time, no matter who criticizes you, no matter how long it takes, no matter how many times you fall.

Get back up again and just keep planting.

About the Author

Adam Khan is the author of the books, *Self-Help Stuff That Works*, *How to Change the Way You Look at Things (in Plain English)*, *Cultivating Fire*, *Antivirus For Your Mind*, *Principles For Personal Growth*, *Direct Your Mind*, *Self-Reliance, Translated*, and *What Difference Does It Make?* He blogs at adamlikhan.com and he's the host of The Adam Bomb podcast.

Adam has been published in Prevention Magazine, Cosmopolitan, Body Bulletin, Your Personal Best Newsletter, Wisdom, Think and Grow Rich Newsletter, the Success Strategies newsletter, and he was a regular columnist for At Your Best (a Rodale Press publication) for seven years where his monthly column was voted the readers' favorite. He has been a regular columnist for Josh Hind's Let's Talk Motivation newsletter and nine other ezines. He's had his work reprinted all over the internet and in others' books all over the world. Write to him at adamkhan@usa.com.

www.ingramcontent.com/pod-product-compliance
Lightning Source LLC
Chambersburg PA
CBHW031446040426
42444CB00007B/990